Dancing in High Cotton

Babette Williams

Enjoy!
Babs

"Dancing in High Cotton," by Babette Williams. ISBN 1-58939-799-1 (soft-cover); 1-58939-800-9 (hardcover).

Published 2005 by Virtualbookworm.com Publishing Inc., P.O. Box 9949, College Station, TX 77842, US. ©2005, Babette Williams. All rights reserved. No part of this publication may be reproduced, stored in a retrieval system, or transmitted in any form or by any means, electronic, mechanical, recording or otherwise, without the prior written permission of Babette Williams.

Manufactured in the United States of America.

In Memory Of

Carol Spencer Mitchell

My Beloved "Middle Girl"

Table of Contents

Acknowledgments 1

Prologue 3

1. The Beginning.. 5

2. The Morning After.. 13

3. Swamp Fever 21

4. Don't Think When It's Raining 29

5. Nothing But the Truth 35

6. Don't Ruffle the Boat 41

7. A Small Private Wedding.................................... 47

8. Now I Lay Me Down to Sleep............................ 59

9. Fifty of One—Half Dozen of Another............. 65

10. Don't Throw Out the Dirty Dishwater
    Until You Have a New Baby 73

11. Woman is a Dog's Best Friend 77

12. Stop the Music—I Want to Get Off 87

13. Never Judge a Rock Star by His Cover 93

14. Snug Harbor.. 105

15. I've Found My Buttons 111

16. God Grant Me Courage............................... 115

17. Old Folks at Home 121

Acknowledgments

To Aubrey, my favorite stubborn, hard-headed old man: Without your love and constant encouragement not a word of this book would have been written, and a strong desire of mine would have been quietly stifled.

My warmest appreciation and thanks to Susan K. Perry, my editor, for her guidance and patience.

And to my entire blended family—you have been part of the story, part of the book's evolving, and the most valued part of my entire life.

Prologue

Looking back, Babs should have paid more attention to the dream.

She'd been having trouble sleeping—but after all, Mike had been dead less than six months, so that was to be expected. The night of the dream she was tossing and turning when Mike suddenly appeared just below the ceiling, floating towards her. He wore a navy blue jacket and crisply pressed gray slacks. But why was Mike, the consummate dandy, wearing a baseball cap, with the visor backwards, for heaven's sake?

Now thoroughly awake, Babs gasped when she realized that Mike, hovering serenely above her, did not have feet. Before she had a chance to catch her breath, Mike stretched out his arms towards her, palms up, and grinned.

"Don't worry, Babs," he said, "you'll be fine." And then he was gone.

I.
The Beginning

I am stretched out on my living room couch enjoying a gin and tonic when the phone rings.

I am bone-tired. How could anyone in their right mind play three sets of tennis and eighteen holes of golf on such an unseasonably hot day in May? Well, it was one way to handle grief. I cuddle my tiny Mini-Dachshund, Dolly, more closely, and am rewarded with a kiss.

The telephone intrudes once again. Although I'm tempted not to answer, by the fourth ring I push off the couch.

"Hello."

It's Kay, co-owner of Mighty Minute Maids, the service that house-cleans for me every Thursday. "What are you doing?" she asks.

"What do you mean, what am I doing? I'm not doing anything. It's almost 8 p.m."

Dancing in High Cotton - 6

"Fine," Kay quickly replies. "Aubrey and I'll pick you up in an hour. We're going dancing at the Ritz." With that, she hung up.

This is ridiculous. Maybe I could get in touch with Kay and tell her I'm not interested in going out. But where was she? There had been lots of noise in the background when Kay phoned—maybe she was at a bar. Aubrey: that must be the "nice widower who loves to dance" who Kay raves about every single Thursday when she comes to clean.

God, what should I do? It looks as though I'm going out. Heading to my closet, I quickly settle on black silk slacks, a white, long-sleeved silk shirt, and a wide metallic silver belt. That's what I would've worn in Princeton, or for that matter, going out on the Plantation. I add a double-strand pearl necklace and pearl-drop earrings. Slipping into low-heeled, black patent-leather shoes, I wonder about the name "Aubrey." It sounds English and quite proper. In one of her "sales pitches" Kate mentioned that Aubrey was a native of Fernandina Beach and that he owns, among other businesses, the Palace Saloon, the oldest bar in Florida.

Fernandina Beach is the small town on Amelia Island where most of the locals live. The fact that this Aubrey person is "nice and loves to dance" is a plus, but I don't

7 - Babette Williams

want to go out on a date—certainly not with a local who probably thinks the weekly Fernandina paper is the height of sophistication. Last week's headline was "Who Stole the Rod and Reel out of Joe's Garage." My home is The Plantation, a gated community on the south end of the island. Most of the residents are retirees from New Jersey, New York and Ohio.

Without a doubt, I shall kill Kay next Thursday when she and her two employees, in their tidy white shorts and tee shirts, come to clean. Not only that, but I'll remind her to stick to her business instead of trying to run a matrimonial service.

Quickly I apply make-up and run a brush through my hair. I know tonight is headed for disaster.

☙❦❧

As the saying goes, there are two sides to every story. What I didn't realize was that Kay had been using every opportunity at the monthly Chamber of Commerce meeting to tell Aubrey about "this cute little widow woman on the Plantation who loves to dance." And this evening Kay seized her chance to play matchmaker. When the Chamber meeting broke up, a small group—including Kay and Aubrey—went to a bar on the beach to have a few drinks and a bite to eat. And that's when Kay telephoned me.

Returning to the table, Kay smiled at Aubrey.

"The good news is that I've just spoken to Babs, and we're going to pick her up in one hour to go dancing at the Ritz."

"I'm not dressed to go to the Ritz," Aubrey protested. "I've got on these junky old clothes I've been wearing all day. And what will I have in common with a lady from Princeton who lives on the Plantation?"

"We can't change plans now. I've already made the date. She's in the shower. We've got to go out there and pick her up."

cXcXcX

Peeking between the slats of my living room blinds, I see headlights. I hope none of my neighbors notice his car. Even though my two-story stucco house is on a secluded cul-de-sac, someone may be out walking their dog, and word spreads fast. I quickly let the blind fall back in place—I don't want anyone to catch me peeking out the window.

Standing in the doorway I see a tall, overweight man get out of his car. Even though the sky is darkening, outside lights illuminate my driveway. Good Lord, the man

9 - Babette Williams

is absolutely dragging his feet. Does he think I'm some kind of ogre? He's practically walking backwards! His shoulders slump and even the corners of his mouth are turned down. Judging by his body language, he's not so thrilled about a blind date, either.

I introduce myself, and he mumbles his name in reply. At least, I think he said his name. It's hard to tell, with his soft voice and Southern accent. Too bad he can't talk more clearly, like a Northerner. I sneak a better look at my date. Yes, Aubrey is tall. Maybe 6'1", definitely overweight, with tousled grayish hair. He's dressed in a dreadful Hawaiian guayabera shirt, over a pair of ancient khaki pants in need of pressing. The shirt is a faded blue with white embroidery, distinguished by red spots that most likely are dried catsup stains. His scuffed brown loafers are badly in need of a shine. He certainly doesn't care about appearance, I think, but I shall try to be civil and adult. I vow again to kill Kay next Thursday. This is going to be worse than I imagined.

Dolly has been sitting quietly at my feet, but now she tries her best to provide an enthusiastic welcome for our visitor. She sits up, lets out small "Woofs," and goes all out to be her most adorable self. Aubrey bends down to pet her, which seems to brighten him up a bit. Obviously Dolly is doing a better job of being hospitable than her mistress. I notice Aubrey's round blue eyes twinkle when he smiles.

Somehow we manage to close my door and walk to his car, an old gray sedan badly in need of a wash. I settle into the front seat, hoping the grease spots and dog hair won't attach themselves to my black slacks. The floor on my side is interesting. I notice several tattered maps, four empty cups, a roll of paper towels and a bottle of sunscreen.

On the way to the Ritz, we attempt to carry on a conversation. Thank heavens it's only a ten-minute ride as we don't understand one word the other utters. He drawls and mumbles and I speak with a clipped twang.

The sprawling six-story Ritz Hotel, barely two years old, feels elegant. As our car pulls up to the hotel, a valet quickly comes around to open my door. Aubrey, moving with surprising agility for a man of his size, is pushing the door handle. He nods pleasantly at the valet, who says, "Evening, Mr. Williams." This is interesting. Does he know the young man?

Aubrey grips my elbow firmly and leads me into the lobby of the Ritz.

As we walk in, a three-piece band is finishing "New York, New York." Aubrey

11 - Babette Williams

exudes politeness and charm as we head towards a group of his friends. They seem glad to see him, but I'm aware that everyone has stopped talking to look me over.

We sit down on the fringe of the group. Aubrey orders drinks. I barely manage to take a few hefty swallows of my bourbon and coke when the music starts. It's a rock and roll favorite of mine, "Mustang Sally."

"Would you care to dance?" Aubrey asks. I nod my head in acceptance. We walk onto the dance floor and the bandleader smiles at Aubrey.

"Good evening, Mr. Williams." I wonder if everyone at the Ritz knows this man.

Aubrey holds out his arms, I walk into them, and within one minute we're rocking and rolling. Although he makes at least two of me, and he definitely has big feet, he's a supple yet masterful leader. "Mustang Sally" is fast, but his signals are firm and clear so I know which way to turn. He "hears" the music. This guy can flat out "get it."

We don't talk—we just enjoy the music and dance. I feel a grin stretch across my face. It's rare to dance with a new partner and effortlessly pick up his rhythm. I look up at Aubrey, and darned if he isn't cute when he smiles. And he is smiling—from ear to ear. Kay is absolutely right—this man can *dance.*

The band moves into a Jimmy Buffet medley and we stay on the floor, feeling more relaxed with each other as we swing to "Cheeseburger in Paradise," "Margaritaville," and "Son of a Son of a Sailor." I glance around and realize we're the only couple still dancing. People are grouped around the dance floor watching us, clapping to the beat of the music.

We dance for more than two hours until I beg for mercy. I can't believe this overweight man is outlasting me, the athlete, on the dance floor.

"Let's take a break," I suggest, afraid that if we don't stop, I may faint.

Aubrey immediately leads me onto the verandah overlooking the ocean. As we settle ourselves on two comfortable deck chairs, the roar of the surf provides a comforting background. We're quiet for a few minutes. Then, although Aubrey doesn't know it for many a month, he wins my heart.

Looking straight into my eyes, he says, "Babs, I am enchanted. Will you do me the honor of going out with me again?"

Truly, there *is* something to be said for a Southerner. Maybe I won't kill Kay after all.

2.
The Morning After

Dolly is nudging my arm with her pointy little nose, her body squinched low on the bed, her tail beating from side to side, rat-tat-tat, on the coverlet. I groan but don't actually move. This poor response forces her to flap her ears violently, which she knows will get my attention.

I'm still in bed, and its 8:30 in the morning! I bolt upright. No wonder Dolly is insistent: She needs to go out. For a moment I am disoriented. Then I remember—Aubrey, the Ritz, drinking, dancing. And getting home after midnight. Admit it, Babs, you had a really good time.

The phone is ringing. "Babs, this is Uncle Will. Are you in mourning?"

I'm confused. The voice sounds just like Aubrey Williams but I don't have an Uncle Will, and who would ask whether I'm in mourning? And then I get it—what he said was "This is Aubrey Williams. How are you this morning?" We talk a few minutes and make a date for Saturday night.

At 7 p.m. Saturday a smiling Aubrey stands at my door. I can't help but notice his crisp, freshly pressed navy blue slacks, blue and white plaid sports shirt (without spots), and shiny black loafers. He reaches into his pocket and produces two dog biscuits for Dolly. Aubrey is now her friend for life. Dolly is fickle, I remind myself.

We both enjoy the evening and agree to spend Sunday together. We're going out to see Oyster Bay, a 900-acre gated community just off the Island. I think his son, Hugh, and Hugh's wife, Anne, live there.

Sunday is a beautiful, clear day, with a slight breeze that masks the high temperature. Aubrey conducts a tour of Oyster Bay that includes the three outlying islands and the undeveloped portions of the land. His pace is slow, almost leisurely. Accustomed to bouncing along, I alter my pace to match his deliberate stride. He points out the dense growth of live oak, hickory and pine trees, the palmettos, and the many species of birds enjoying a three-acre pond. Aubrey's expertise about plants and birds is impressive. I am painfully aware of my limited knowledge, but my worry is pointless.

15 - Babette Williams

Two days later a book on local flora and fauna is delivered to my house. It's a gift from Aubrey, with a note, "Welcome to Florida."

At the end of the tour we head for Hugh and Anne's home. There's a party going on—maybe "shindig" is a better description. I meet Hugh and Anne, and Hugh's sister, Debbie, who is a lawyer, and her husband, Walt, a pediatrician. We walk behind Hugh's home to join about twenty others in the back yard.

Without thinking, I sniff the air because there's a strong, pungent aroma coming from somewhere. Hugh notices, gives me a crooked grin, and leads me to a huge pot that is hanging over a propane gas fire.

"We're having a low country boil," he explains. "It's a spicy, highly seasoned Cajun dish. Here, come here, let me show you."

I peek in the pot—I'm not much for highly seasoned food—and see shrimp, crabs, clams, sausage, corn, and potatoes simmering in sauce. Hugh hands me a ladle and paper plate.

"Come on," he urges. "Try some. It's really good."

Debbie tells me the family owns Oyster Bay. This is a surprise, but I'm beginning to learn that Aubrey is unassuming, a man very comfortable in his own skin. Everyone talks southern—just like Aubrey. They add extra syllables to many of the words, making it hard for a northern person to always understand. For instance, my sister's name is "Joyce." Down here it's pronounced, "Joy-ace." I guess you could say they drawl.

I've never been to a low country boil before. It's not like any picnic I've ever known. The food is different, and somehow the atmosphere seems more laid-back and casual. Hugh brings out a guitar, Aubrey starts plunking a uke, and Debbie and a few guests begin to sing along. Even if I did know the songs I wouldn't have recognized the words—not how *they* sang them.

When we get home, I thank Aubrey and tell him I'll be busy next week, as my daughter, Carol, and her fiancé, Mitch, are arriving tomorrow.

"That's fine, Babs," he says. "I'll call."

ⱯⱯⱯ

Carol, Brian, and I spend a busy Memorial Day catching up on their plans. I tell them about Aubrey.

"He's different, very Southern and sort of a good old boy." All at once I realize he has kept me thoroughly occupied the last five days.

17 - Babette Williams

"I'm glad to see you perky again, Mom," Carol comments.

The next evening we go to Sonny's Restaurant, as Brian has a yen for barbecued ribs. Leaving the restaurant, I see Aubrey talking to some man in the parking lot.

"That's Aubrey," I say, pointing to him.

The next thing I know she's with Aubrey, and they appear to be having an animated conversation. I've been standing next to our car with Brian, but decide to join them, and am astounded to hear Carol invite Aubrey to dinner the following evening.

"I was planning to take you and Brian to the Verandah, Carol."

She doesn't miss a beat. Smiling sweetly, she turns to Aubrey, "Surely you'll join us?" We say our good-byes and get in the car.

"Carol, have you gone mad?"

Carol, always quick to read other people, tells me, "Mother, this is a nice man. A very nice man. I like him, and you need to know him better."

The four of us have dinner at the Verandah on the Plantation, and Aubrey casually mentions that he once owned the stores at the resort. This man is full of surprises. He probably would never have brought it up, but it seems as though everybody at the Verandah comes over to say hello.

The next evening Aubrey plans to show us the town—and he does. We have hors d'oeuvres at one place, the main course at an Italian restaurant, and end up at the Palace, drinking Pirate's Punch and dancing like four crazy people. I don't know when I've had so much fun.

When we get back to my house, Brian and Carol go inside, and Aubrey suggests he and I go for a little walk. The air feels good, and we stroll along the darkened street holding hands. It's a very comfortable feeling.

On our way back, Aubrey leans down and pulls me close, whispering into my ear, "Oh, this feels so familiar—you feel just right." He hugs me tightly, his mouth finds mine, and we're kissing. I feel breathless, surprised, and elated, all at the same time. After a few minutes, reluctantly, we break apart.

"Aubrey," I ask him, "When you say I feel familiar, do I remind you of Pat?" I already know that Pat died recently after 38 years of marriage. He nods slowly. "She was a petite lady, feisty, like you." He's silent, remembering.

My heart fills with warmth for this lady I never met, a woman who inspired this man to the deepest sort of commitment. We

19 - Babette Williams

amble towards my house, holding hands, and I understand Aubrey's beginning to like me a lot. And maybe I'm beginning to like him more than I'm willing to admit.

He breaks the silence. "What does "Babs" stand for?"

"My given name is Babette," I tell him.

"That's a pretty name. Would you mind if I call you Babette?"

I'm startled, but, hey, what does it matter? "No, that's fine with me. Babette it is."

He's a serious man. I decide to speak. "Aubrey, there are three things you need to know about me before we go any further." He is listening attentively, so I go on.

"The first thing is that I'm not a rich widow."

He thinks for a minute and replies, "Babette, on paper I'm probably very comfortable, but I'm not rich, either."

Satisfied, I continue. "The second thing is, I've learned that I'm three years older than you."

Aubrey looks at me and says, "So? Who gives a damn at our age?" I can tell he truly means just that, so I ask the final question.

"And the third thing is, I'm part Jewish."

He looks at me reflectively and asks, "Can you make chicken soup?"

3.

Swamp Fever

I should have listened more carefully when Aubrey confided that he was a dyed-in-the-wool Florida "Gator." We were talking about sports, which I love, and he asked if I like football. I nodded eagerly and told him yes, I do.

Per usual, we are unaware there is a communication problem. How could we know? We've only been dating a few months. Besides that, we're in our sixties, and I'm from Princeton, New Jersey, and he's a good ole Southern boy.

I am picturing Ivy League football, carefully orchestrated tailgate parties, elegant cocktail parties and casual chic. Aubrey is thinking of SEC football—huge crowds, a do-or-die atmosphere and a hell-bent-for-leather team. No chic. We said no more about it. He didn't know I didn't have the slightest conception of football in the

Dancing in High Cotton - 22

south. I didn't know the *only* sport Aubrey cared about was Florida football.

Aubrey gave another clear message when he insisted we make a special trip to Gainesville two weeks before the first game so he could take me shopping for Gator clothes. I believe his exact words were, "to properly outfit me for The Swamp."

I didn't know, and didn't think to ask, about The Swamp because I was indignant at the implication that my clothes weren't suitable. After all, I was quite sure I'd always been considered a chic and stylish dresser. Football games took place in Princeton, too. A woman wore a strictly tailored suit, medium high heels with stockings, and a fur coat once the weather turned cold. For fun, she might throw an orange and black striped wool Princeton scarf around her neck. Of course, I haven't been to a football game in forty years.

We visited six stores before I settled on two white shirts with tiny alligator emblems. They were hard to find among the stock in the clothing stores—everything was orange and blue. I could tell Aubrey was disappointed in my taste because he kept shoving tacky orange and blue shirts at me, but I kept refusing to buy them.

Today is the first game of the season. It's only 8:30 in the morning, and I'm watching Aubrey, clad in blue slacks, an

23 - Babette Williams

orange-and-blue-striped shirt and white sneakers, carefully attach Gator decals to the front doors of his brand new white Chrysler LHS. Then he selects just the right decals for the rear of the car and the hood. I can't help thinking how grateful I am that the entire car isn't painted orange, or even blue trimmed with big orange stripes. *He probably hasn't thought of it. I'll never mention the idea.* As if that isn't enough, he adds a two-foot orange wind tunnel flag on each side of the car, securing them with a vise on each back window.

He disappears into his house, returning moments later with a huge cooler. "For the tail-gate party," he explains, on his way back inside. Seconds later he reappears carrying two large canvas bags filled with booze, Seven-Up, soda water, tonic water, Pepsi, Coke, and orange and blue paper cups with the University of Florida logo.

While this is going on, a tape blares out school songs "so we'll get in the mood," Aubrey confides, smiling from ear to ear. He is clearly happy, excited, and anxious to begin the two-hour trip to Gainesville. I check my watch, and it's just 8:45 a.m. I guess we're going to party for a *long* time.

As we near Gainesville, traffic becomes bumper to bumper, and I see that every single car is decked out with signs and logos, just like ours. Aubrey's waving at the other drivers, and having a good old time. I'm getting this slight sinking feeling in the pit of my stomach.

"I can't wait to get to The Swamp," Aubrey says. "Nobody gets out alive." I can only hope he means the opposing football team.

We stop at Popeye's to pick up 120 pieces of chicken, three dozen biscuits, and three pounds of rice. "So we can party," he explains as we get back in the car and head for the campus. Aubrey turns left and right on the narrow college streets, dodging between long lines of parked cars and backed-up traffic. He pulls into the driveway of a neat bungalow on Twentieth Drive.

The scene is as bewildering to me as the Low Country Boil at Hugh's house. His friends are busy opening car trunks and setting up a buffet on two long picnic tables in front of the house. Dave and his wife, Nita, brought home cooked ribs; Jack and Zee made a huge salad; we are amply prepared with 120 pieces of chicken and a mountain of rice; and Allen and Nancy contribute devilled eggs. Drinks are served, if that's the right expression, from the trunks of the cars.

I notice that every single person, male and female, is decked out in orange and blue.

25 - Babette Williams

Two hours later, stuffed with food and feeling quite mellow, we're on the way to the stadium. Aubrey has been clear that we need to arrive early so we won't miss anything. He holds my elbow as we plod up the ramp for the first game of the season, shoulder to shoulder with other loyal fans, carrying our binoculars, headsets, water bottles, fans and programs.

At exit seven, we leave the ramp to enter the stadium. Gamely I follow Aubrey as we struggle up the concrete steps to the very top row of seats where we collapse next to his daughter, Debbie, and son-in-law, Walt. I think about suggesting he change the tickets for next year, but Aubrey informs me proudly that it has taken him over 25 years to work up to these seats.

The temperature is at least 95 degrees. I sip my Evian water as sweat pours down the neck of my inappropriate plain white tee shirt. We watch both teams warm up, the cheerleaders warm up, the stadium fill to capacity, and finally—forty-five minutes later—the team trots out of the tunnel.

I sense a violent movement next to me and turn to see Aubrey on his feet, screaming at the top of his lungs, "GO GATORS!" I look around the stadium and am amazed to see 85,000 people doing the same thing! I sit in my seat. There is a lot to absorb.

Dancing in High Cotton - 26

Five minutes into the game the Gators score their first touchdown. The Swamp goes crazy! Once again every single person in the Gator section of the stadium jumps up screaming, "GO, GATORS!" Aubrey turns to me and gives me a huge kiss on the lips. His daughter, Debbie, turns to me and we high-five. The people in front of us turn around and we exchange more high-fives. I guess kissing or high-fiving depends on the depth of personal relationship.

I compare this bedlam to the rare occasions Princeton managed to score, resulting in a weak "rah rah" and a polite smattering of applause. Now I understand why Princeton seldom made the Top Ten.

I never actually see much of that first game. I'm hot, tired, stuffed, cranky, and I have a stiff neck from watching Aubrey, the Raging Maniac. I don't care about the behavior of the other 85,000 fans, but I do care how Aubrey conducts himself. After all, we've only been dating three months, and I'm still checking him out. Is the man so rabid about everything, or is it just Florida football? Maybe he's a total lunatic in other situations and will embarrass me forevermore. And what if he decides I'm a fuddy-duddy? Not that I don't have strong passions, too. I love tennis tournaments, but spectators express their appreciation in a more sedate fashion.

27 - Babette Williams

That night, after I settle down in my own peaceful house, I call each of my three daughters and tell them about the bizarre events of the day. I feel clean and marginally refreshed after a long hot shower, and am enjoying the aftermath of an extra tall, strong gin and tonic. This drinking could become habit forming, I think, as I try to convey my impressions of Florida football in a clear and orderly fashion to the girls.

My daughters ask concise, penetrating questions: "What's he like? Do you think this is a mismatch? Do you love him?"

The next evening my eldest daughter calls and says she and her sibs had a conference. They feel it's quite clear I have to pass the football test with Aubrey if I want this relationship to continue. I'm not completely sure, but I'm learning Aubrey is awesome in so many ways—yes, he's worth adapting for.

Now three games have come and gone. I guess I've passed the test with flying colors—orange and blue, to be exact. I have a closet full of orange and blue shirts, shorts, slacks, sweaters, and shoes, all with large gator designs.

Aubrey today called each of my daughters to tell them I am a true Gator fan, and that he is very pleased. It seems that at the University of Florida-Mississippi game yesterday, after the referee made a bad call, I jumped up and yelled, "What's the matter with you, you *&%$#!"

Today he proposed, and I accepted. He surely thought I would, because when I said "yes," he whipped a jewelry box out of his jacket pocket. I was quite delighted, but not entirely surprised, to find a pair of large gold earrings shaped like gators, and a matching gold necklace with a hanging gator pendant. Oh yes, we're going to pick out a ring when we both have more time, probably after football season.

Post Script:

Although I didn't know it then, 1993 was the perfect time to be introduced to Florida football. It was the beginning of the "Wuerffel House" years, starring Danny Wuerffel, the fantastic quarterback, and a talented team. In 1996 we were among the fortunate Gators that partied in New Orleans when we won the National Championship. Over time I've become a staunch fan—even our dogs sport Gator collars. And now, twelve football seasons later, we've moved into Oak Hammock at the University, and our seats are in the new Club Section.

4.
Don't Think When It's Raining

I should have taken Aubrey's proposal more seriously. Even though Aubrey's the marrying kind, it's only September; we've known each other five months—too soon for me to consider marriage. Aubrey and I are having so much fun together. Perhaps it's best for this relationship to continue just the way it is. Maybe the reason it's *so* enjoyable is that we're *not* husband and wife.

Aubrey has suggested I move in with him when my house sells. He points out we'd have an easier time finding our clothes. Seems as though I'm leaving more and more stuff at Aubrey's and then I wonder why a certain belt, or pair of shoes, isn't in my own closet. Up until now I've shrugged off the possibility of living together. I want my independence, and I'm not eager to drift into a situation that may be uncomfortable. We don't know each other well enough to know whether our personalities will mesh on a long-term basis. What if it doesn't work out? What a mess that would be!

Besides, I'm not sure I'll stay on Amelia Island. I'm not sure about Aubrey. For the past two months, ever since I put my house on the market, I've been looking at property on the Island and also in Sarasota, near my sister. And now here I sit with a contract for this house in my hand. The realtor just left, and I'm stunned because the prospective buyers want to take possession within 30 days. Whether I like it or not, it's decision time.

I'm not sure, as wonderful as Aubrey appears to be, whether I'm willing to become Mrs. Aubrey Williams.

He'll be here in a few minutes—we need to talk about all this. And what will my children say if I *do* move in with him?

There he is now. I can't wait to shove the contract into his hand. He puts his granny glasses on and studies the document for a few minutes.

"Well, that settles it. You'll just move in with me. There's nothing to think about." It's easy for *him* to say.

"Aubrey,"—I want to phrase this softly— "have you ever considered the possibility that we won't be happy together? That one

31 - Babette Williams

or the other of us will decide this is not workable?"

Aubrey's face assumes a quizzical look. Then he brightens. "It's really simple, Babette. If that's the case, I'll just help you pack, we'll find a house or apartment that you like, and I'll help you get resettled."

I have a flash of intuition and absolutely *know* that Aubrey means exactly that. "Well," I'm surprised to hear myself say, "let's start packing."

Three weeks later, Dolly and I move to Highland Drive.

Have you ever noticed that dogs adjust more readily than humans? It didn't take Dolly long to discover that her new life promised to be far superior to her old, mundane existence on Sparkleberry Drive. Her first eye-opener was in the culinary department. Aubrey believes in allowing his dogs to eat when they're hungry. He sees to it that their two oversized aluminum bowls are filled to the brim with dog food at all times. One hour after our arrival, Aubrey places a third bowl next to the others.

"Aubrey," I protest, "Dolly is a *little* dog. She usually eats about twenty kernels of dry dog food once a day. This bowl is bigger than she is. Do you want to kill her?"

"Don't give it a second thought, Babette." He fills up the third bowl with dry food. "It may take her a few weeks, but she'll adjust to having food whenever she wants, and she won't overeat." Not wanting to argue just one hour after my arrival, I nod. With a sinking feeling, I observe my tiny dog bury her entire face in the bowl (which is indeed bigger than she is).

Two hours later Aubrey removes Dolly's collar, tossing it carelessly in a drawer. I'll probably never see it again.

"Why did you do that?" I ask.

"She won't need a leash. Tomoka will teach her to go in and out the dog doors by herself, and the yard is fenced. She'll have total freedom."

Tomoka, one of Aubrey's two German Shepherds, has been watching Dolly intently. I sense that this is the exact moment when the stately Shepherd decides Dolly's a puppy and adopts her. This is a full-time chore, and Tomoka takes her new duties as a mother seriously. We watch as she herds Dolly from place to place. Occasionally, Dolly objects to being mothered and snaps viciously at Tomoka, getting a big mouthful of hair for her troubles. Tomoka's expression is quizzical. She seems to think her "puppy" is simply silly and favors her with a "What, are you *crazy?*" expression. Then she proceeds to lick her baby from head to foot.

So, within two hours, Dolly has a mother and all the food she wants. She's in doggy heaven.

33 - Babette Williams

I'm not doing nearly as well. Either I have too large a wardrobe, or closet space is too severely limited. I open the large walk-in closet in the master bedroom. It's crammed with Aubrey's clothes. I slam the door shut and make a mental note that this closet has to be straightened within a week. How can the poor man even get dressed in the morning?

"Aubrey,"—very firmly—"there's no room for my belongings in your closet."
I see his expression and soften. "Never mind, I'll just use the guest room closets for now."

Confidently, I open the seven-foot closet in one bedroom. It's packed. I don't think there's room for one pair of my shortest shorts. I go to the other room. It's worse. Quickly, I close that closet door too. This is becoming a teensy problem. Stay calm, I tell myself. This is a big house with lots of closets (though all seem to be stuffed and messy). Surely there's a place for my clothes somewhere.

Frustrated, I go into the bathroom I'll share with Aubrey. I open every drawer, every cabinet, and the linen closet. There's not an inch of free space. I've never seen so much of everything—such chaos. Why didn't I notice this when I stayed over before? Why does he need twelve J & J baby powders? And soap—twenty bars—

maybe he represents the soap company. He likes Zest. I like Dove.

This is a nightmare. And I've been here less than three hours. I want to go home.

5.
Nothing But the Truth

It's exactly two months ago today that I moved to Highland Drive. I'm checking the days off on a calendar tacked to the refrigerator, which sounds as though I think of this as a prison sentence, and that's not quite the case.

It took Dolly, my erstwhile buddy, less than two weeks to desert me in favor of her *new* canine friends. Instead of following *me* around, she now hangs out with Tomoka. She hasn't got an ounce of loyalty in that fat, fat, fat body of hers. As I predicted the day we moved in, Dolly no longer weighs seven and a half pounds. She doesn't walk: she waddles, resembling a sausage with little black toothpicks for legs. I bet she weighs over *ten* pounds. However, I must admit she's already beginning to lose the excess weight as Aubrey predicted. It's finally dawning on her that food bowls will always be full, scraps will be divided evenly, and best of all, the big dogs will move out of her way to let her have whatever she wants from any bowl.

As for me, I feel as though I'm on a roller coaster. I'm no longer a sensible, calm and capable adult. I admit my behavior at times is downright childish. But then, so is his. Aubrey is a mellow man—almost nothing bothers him. He wants me to be happy, and the only time he's out of sorts is when I'm discontented. The problem is, he's so mellow and laid-back that nothing gets accomplished.

There's so much we could do—clean the garage, empty closets, redecorate the house—my list goes on and on. Aubrey says he agrees that these tasks need to be done. It's just that we have trouble with the time frame. I'm a *now* person—Aubrey's a *whenever* person.

A small poem I learned as a kid keeps running around in my head. "Rabbits have habits, and we do, too. The problem is, ours are askew."

On the other hand, we have so much fun that I've begun to wonder about little things, like neatness. Do they really matter? Aubrey says I clean off the table before he's finished with his meal. He's getting very stubborn about holding onto his coffee mug with both hands.

37 - Babette Williams

Today, with Aubrey's complete approval, I'm going to straighten the cabinets in our bathroom.

"We're going to be sharing now," I told him, "and I need space for my toiletries."

"Go ahead, honey," he agreed. "But please don't throw anything away before I see it."

"I wouldn't think of it," I replied with confidence. "I'll just make a pile of things I'm not sure about."

In a burst of enthusiasm and buoyed with the idea of a neat and tidy bathroom, I empty all the cabinets and the linen closet, and clear the top of the counter. I decide to dump everything on the floor. I knew the cabinets were chock full, but this is ridiculous. I count seven *open* Johnson and Johnson talcum powders, dozens of assorted bandages, three hot water bottles, every kind of vitamin, more medicines than I knew existed—all in a jumble. How did he ever *find* anything?

"It's good to have everything you need at home," he explained to me many times when I asked why we needed fourteen jars of pickles, for instance.

After several hours Aubrey peeks around the door, and I assure him, "I haven't thrown one thing away. This pile is for you to check out. It has mostly old and outdated medicines from years ago." I smile, he smiles, both of us contented.

Two more hours pass. Stiff but happy, I struggle to get off the floor. I have just finished a mammoth reorganization. I know Aubrey will love the neat cabinets, with all the products perfectly aligned.

"Aubrey, come see. Wait till you see the closet!"

Smiling, he looks around appreciatively. "Boy, you've been a busy lady."
I beam.

"By the way, have you seen a box of Metamucil? It's crumpled looking."

My heart sinks. I know we have a problem. "What is Metamucil? I don't think I've seen such an item."

"You know," Aubrey says. "It's a green and white, small square box, but it would be crumpled up."

"No, I don't think I've seen anything like that."

"What day is today? Oh, it's Thursday. I'll be right back. I have to check the garbage." Aubrey flies out the door. I cannot figure out why Metamucil is so important. Why is he checking the garbage?

In ten minutes Aubrey is back, looking crest-fallen. "It was too late—the garbage has been picked up."

39 - Babette Williams

I still don't get it. After a minute's silence Aubrey confides. "Well, you see, I kept $400 hidden in the Metamucil box."

"Aubrey, that's horrible. Four hundred dollars! I'm so, so very sorry." I feel ill. Nobody throws away $400, but I just did.

"It's all right, honey," Aubrey says. "After all, I didn't tell you to watch for a Metamucil box. It's my fault." Aubrey opens his arms and reaches out to hug me.

There is nothing better than an Aubrey hug.

But the Metamucil episode isn't closed. Aubrey has a second thought. "What I really mean is, I shouldn't have believed you when you said you wouldn't throw anything out."

6.

Don't Ruffle the Boat

It seems as though every time I make a suggestion, it leads to trouble.

"It's a beautiful day," I ventured one lovely morning. "Your canoe's been sitting down at the dock for ages, and you just bought a new motor for it. Why don't we use it?"

"That's a great idea," Aubrey agrees. "Let's do it." Within a few minutes we change into sneakers and grungies so we can enjoy our new toy. Quickly I toss together a few sandwiches, fix a thermos of iced tea, and put them in a tote bag along with plastic cups, chips, pickles, peppers, and paper towels. In ten minutes, I'm ready.

Aubrey sensibly decides to use a little four-wheel dolly to transport the motor. This is a good idea, since Egan's Creek is about 500 feet down a grassy incline behind our house, and the motor is heavy and cumbersome. The two of us finally manage to get the motor on the dolly, and we head down the hill. Aubrey is alternately pulling and pushing the dolly, depending on the terrain, while I try to keep the motor centered. Finally, after struggling down the hill, we unload the motor onto the dock. Both of us are perspiring, ever so slightly.

We trudge back up the hill. I never realized how far the dock was: it's a steep climb to the house. Aubrey picks up the gas tank, a new line to replace the old rope, and the paddles, and starts down the hill. I lug the tote bag full of goodies. We congratulate ourselves when we get to the dock.

Oops! We forgot the life jackets. Back up the hill. Neither of us is sure where they're stowed, so we both hunt for them. Ten minutes later, our search has not turned up even one life jacket.

Then Aubrey remembers, "Oh, I think they're on our boat." (We have a 24-footer at our dock that we haven't used in a year.) We trudge back down the hill. I'm very sweaty (I'm past perspiring) and look forward to being on the boat, enjoying the cool breeze.

Aubrey turns the canoe upright, and I help him mount the motor. Satisfied that it's attached securely, he gently eases the boat over the side of the dock. He's got a

43 - Babette Williams

strong grip on the rope with his right hand so that the canoe won't drift off once it hits the water. As the boat slips into the creek, the frayed rope gives way. The canoe is now loose, moving down the creek with the tide.

Aubrey watches the canoe, the frayed rope in his hand, as it slowly drifts away from us. I watch Aubrey, waiting for instructions. After all, he's the boater, and I'm the landlubber. I try to keep our roles straight. Five minutes pass, ever so slowly. I can't believe he still isn't doing anything.

"Aubrey, Aubrey," I try to speak softly, just like he does. "We need to get the canoe."

"I know, Babette," he says in an overly patient tone, "but first I want to see if it lands at our neighbor's dock."

It seems as though it's forever, for I'm a believer in instant action, but it's most likely only five more minutes until the boater speaks again.

"Shit," he says softly.

Even I can figure out that the canoe is now firmly aground on a mud bank. (Egan's Creek is tidal so mud banks are exposed at low tide.) Reluctantly, Aubrey sits on the edge of the dock and removes his shoes. It dawns on me that my darling is going into the water.

"Aubrey," I ask in a fearful tone, "aren't there *alligators* in the creek?"

"Yes, there are lots of them, but I haven't seen any today," he reassures me.

Now I'm downright worried. What if there *is* an alligator, and he just didn't notice? He looks around, doesn't spy anybody (I guess this includes alligators), strips off his pants, and slides off the dock into the ice-cold water. The creek isn't deep—probably about six feet—but it sure is muddy. I watch in fascination.

Aubrey starts to swim. He's an excellent swimmer, having grown up on the beach, but he's having a hard time making any progress. Being coated with mud is definitely a deterrent to speed. Aubrey reminds me of a walrus wallowing on a muddy bank.

I can't help it. The laughter rises up, and I can't contain it. All thoughts about alligators leave my mind, erased by the sight of Aubrey, the walrus. I am doubled up, wishing I could share this moment. If I only had a camera—this is a real Candid Camera sequence—to capture this image forever. There he is, swimming the side-stroke, inching towards the canoe, which at least is at a standstill, mired in mud.

Finally Aubrey catches up with the elusive vessel. He attempts to swing over the edge into it very carefully, so it won't tip. The problem is magnified because he's so slippery from the mud that every time he

45 - Babette Williams

tries to swing over the edge, he loses his grip and falls back into the water. Not only that, but now the canoe is coated with mud, making it even more difficult to get aboard. On the fifth attempt he manages to swing a leg over, followed by the rest of his filthy, mud-covered self.

Silently, he paddles back to the dock. I throw him the new line, which he attaches to the boat. I grab the rope and fasten it securely to the dock. In a second Aubrey is safe ashore.

We now have two problems: we have to clean the boat, and Aubrey needs to put on his clothes. It's really not polite to be seen in your jockey shorts in public.

Aubrey shakes some mud off, but it's useless. He stands still for a moment, indecisive, then says, "Damned if I'm going to do all this work and not go for a ride!"
He pulls on his pants over the mud-coated shorts, and climbs back into the boat. He offers me his hand, and I join him. He starts the motor and we putt slowly away. I wish my tote bag had something stronger than iced tea.

Ignoring the mud, I reach over and give my hero a great big hug and messy kiss, careful not to tip the canoe. There may be alligators lurking in the creek.

7.
A Small Private Wedding

"Babette, it's time for us to get married!"

We're strolling down Centre Street on our way to lunch. I stop in my tracks to absorb this idea. I expected we'd get married—I just didn't think it would be quite this soon.

Immediately I picture our wedding. It will be an elegant affair—the type of wedding I'm accustomed to attending in Princeton. I'll wear a cocktail-length beige dress, while Aubrey will most likely choose a navy blue suit. Although he hates ties, this is one time he'll have to wear one. A 5:00 p.m. ceremony for family and a few close friends, followed by cocktails and dinner—oh, this is so exciting!

"You're right, Aubrey, it's time." I nod my head vigorously. "I suppose the first step is to work on a guest list."

We've reached the Marina, and as soon as we're comfortably settled at a table, I pull out a memo pad and pencil. (I can produce almost anything from my Vera Maxwell oversize tote.) We start a guest list, believing, in our infinite naiveté, that this will be a ten-minute procedure. We know we'll invite our children, my sister and brother-in-law, and a few close friends. Quickly I scrawl the names of the children, their spouses, my sister and brother-in-law. Now it's time to decide on "close friends."

"Let's start with out-of-towners first," suggests Aubrey, "then the locals, the Plantation, and the football crowd."

"Good idea," I nod, pushing the pencil as quickly as I can, trying to keep up with the people that are popping into my head. I look up. Aubrey's watching me closely. He hasn't said a word, and I've covered one memo page with names.

"Okay, it's your turn," I say expectantly.

Aubrey rattles off a dozen couples, filling a second memo page (they're just little-bitty sheets). I decide to count.

"Aubrey," I gasp, "would you believe we've listed 20 relatives, counting cousin Billy, twelve couples from New Jersey and ten people from Alabama. That's over 50 people, and we've barely gotten started. Maybe we should consider other possibilities. How would you feel about eloping?"

We're quiet for a moment, contemplating the consequences of going off to be married without telling our children. It won't do.

49 - Babette Williams

"I don't think we should do that," we say simultaneously. There's no discussion, because it's clearly not an option.

"You know, Babette," says Aubrey, picking his words carefully, "we need to decide what we want to happen at our wedding. I'm thinking it should be a wonderful party to celebrate a joyous occasion: two old people who found each other and decide to get married. It needs to be *a party*, not a solemn event."

Aubrey's right. We can have an elegant private ceremony for family, just as I've pictured, followed by a wingding celebration a few days later. It's a perfect plan.

"I see your point. Well, maybe we should have a quiet ceremony for just the family, followed by a big celebration for everyone."

Our lunch arrives. I put away the memos and we dig in. We're both pleased with our decisions.

That evening we compile the final guest list. The stumbling block seems to be friends. We have a lot of friends. We each make separate lists. We end up with Aubrey's close friends, not so close friends, questionable friends, and people he is obligated to include, as well as Babette's close friends, not so close friends, questionable friends and obligations. After paring the list to the bone, we end up with 275 people. We are in shock.

This is a small island, and there are only a few places equipped to handle 275 guests. We eliminate the Ritz and the Women's Club as too formal, the 1878 Steak House and Walker's Landing at the Plantation as too small, and Ten Acres as too rustic. We discuss the possibilities of every single restaurant in town. We're at a standstill. Then Aubrey has a brainstorm.

"Let's have the party at the Palace Saloon," he suggests. "We probably can use the large back room on a Sunday, and size-wise it would be perfect." Since Aubrey has owned the Palace for many years, I trust his judgment regarding the ability of the Palace to cope with 275 guests. He makes one phone call to the manager, and it's done. Now we have a guest list, and a place to have our party. All we need to do is choose a date, and we'll be all set.

The next morning I begin to ruminate about the guest list. Did we remember everyone? Maybe we should include more people at the ceremony? Where should we have the ceremony? Good heavens, we have to have a band. How can you have a wingding party without a great band? Maybe we're not so set after all.

In the evening we join a group of friends at a local hangout, the 1878 Steak House. As we walk into the bar, a steel drum player and a guitarist are playing one of our favorite Jimmy

51 - Babette Williams

Buffett numbers, "Margaritaville." We go directly to the dance floor—the band's rhythm is terrific. As we twist and turn to the music, Aubrey and I exchange knowing glances. We'll hire the "Smiling Islanders" to play at our party.

The Islanders' only available date is Sunday, June 26th, which is less than two months away. Their next opening would be October, and that won't do as it's football season. I've always wanted to be a June bride. This time I'll get my wish.

Relieved that we have a party date, we now need a date and place to have our wedding ceremony. I'm having trouble with this.

"Aubrey, I'm concerned about assembling five sets of children, each with their own schedules, for the wedding ceremony and again, possibly within a week or two, for the party. Ellen's in Aspen, Debbie's in Tallahassee, Carol's in Israel, and Sue's in New Jersey. The only one who can easily make both events will be Hugh."

Aubrey nods somberly. "Let's have another drink and discuss this." Which we do for well over an hour, going round and round, not arriving at any plan that makes sense.

Maybe the simplest solution is to elope. Heck, the kids know we're going to marry. If there's a choice, I'd rather have them at the party, anyway. So much for marrying at the Ritz in a beautiful beige dress.

On the way home from the Steak House, Aubrey and I agree that during the next few weeks we'll slip out of town and get married.

Next we put our minds to designing a unique invitation. I will admit that what we came up with might possibly be considered gaudy. The front of the card sports a large "Gator" dressed in an orange and blue tuxedo and top hat. The message inside is straightforward:

Come celebrate the marriage of

Babette Spencer

and

Aubrey Williams

Sunday, June 26, 1994

3:00 P.M.

Dancing to an island band

*

No ties for men, no heels for women

We enclose a stamped, addressed postcard with a color photo of the Palace Saloon on the cover. On the reverse side, a

53 - Babette Williams

Gator holds a signboard, "Yes, I can come; No, I must miss it." All the invitees have to do is sign their name and slip the postcard in the mail.

A few weeks later, exactly one month ahead of time, we mail the invitations. Now all we have to do is wait.

And the postcards pour in. Everyone wants to celebrate our marriage. Two weeks before THE DAY, Aubrey and I meet with Jimmy, the Palace Manager. In place of one buffet table we'll have serving stands in different areas so that people will mill around. We settle on a large shrimp bar, a roast beef stand, a pasta and cheese stand, and two full-service bars. Waitresses will pass hot hors d'oeuvres and the landmark drink of the Palace, Pirate's Punch.

Our five sets of married children keep wanting to know the date we got married. We smile and tell them the truth, which is that we'll announce it at our party.

It's ten days until the big event and Aubrey and I still haven't married. How can we celebrate our marriage if we aren't married? We need to do something quickly. I have a brilliant inspiration.

"Wait a minute—it's not a problem. We'll just marry at the Palace in front of 275 of our nearest and dearest."

I have this fleeting thought, which I dismiss immediately. My sister, who is in her late seventies—what will she think about her baby sister being married on a SUNDAY in a SALOON? Can't think about this—we have other issues to solve.

Who will perform the ceremony? We call Debbie, Aubrey's daughter, and ask her to do the honors. She holds almost every degree offered by the University of Florida: she's a lawyer, mortgage broker, real estate broker, and most importantly, a notary public. In Florida you may officiate at a wedding if you're a certified notary public. Crazy, but true.

Debbie is a person who considers all consequences. She asks for a few days to think it over. While she thinks, we stew about what to do if she refuses, as time is running out. Finally Debbie tells us, "I married my brother, and now I'll marry my father." We ask her not to tell a soul.

What we have now is a *surprise wedding.* This party is shaping up to be a *real* wingdinger.

Seven days before the event I'm still in a quandary about what to wear. Aubrey is planning on white slacks with a red and white Hawaiian print shirt. Easy for him— he's male. I want to look like a bride, but this party is being held on a Sunday afternoon at a saloon. What does one wear to be married in a bar?

55 - Babette Williams

So much for the elegant wedding, the tea-length beige silk dress, the pearls, the sophistication.

A shopping trip to nearby St. Simon's Island turns up a pair of beige silk slacks, matching silk blouse trimmed with sequins and a wide beige hemp belt which seems to be dressy enough for a bride yet suitable for an island party. It's the best I can do.

Aubrey and I decide to prepare nametags, even though it's not usually done at a private party. We agree that one of our daughters will stand at the door to hand them out as people arrive. On Friday, Ellen, my eldest, volunteers to hand out the nametags. We explain that the tags are arranged in alphabetical groups: the out-of-towners, the locals, and the relatives, for easy reference. As folks walk through the door, all she has to do is find out where they're from and their name. Ellen assures us she can deal with this effectively, and we shouldn't worry about it. She's in her mid-forties—we leave it to her to handle. This turns out to be a mistake.

We order a three-tiered wedding cake for delivery at 3 p.m. on Sunday. Aubrey and I are ready.

On Friday our guests start to arrive from all over the United States: Texas, Montana, Pennsylvania, New York, New Jersey, and Florida. We've reserved a group of rooms at Shoney's, the only motel on the island. We put a large welcome package in each room that includes directions to the Palace and plans for Friday and Saturday nights.

Art Elzroth, an old friend of Aubrey's, heads the Texas contingent. He invites all the out-of-towners to a huge bash at the Crab Trap on Friday evening. Everyone is in high spirits—actually downright rowdy. The big question of the evening: "When did you get married?" Each time it's asked, we just grin and look smug.

The following evening Hugh and Anne host a buffet dinner at their home. Again, we're quite a rowdy crew, dancing, telling jokes, and cutting up.

It's Sunday. AUBREY AND I ARE GETTING MARRIED TODAY.

We get to the Palace for a last-minute check of the food stations *and* the bars. Precisely at 3:00, our guests begin to descend in droves. The band is playing, drinks are being distributed freely, hors d'oeuvres are being passed—the atmosphere is upbeat. This shindig is off to a good start.

We hear a commotion at the door. The entrance is backed up with people waiting to get into the party. What on earth is wrong? Ellen doesn't seem to be there . . . Where is she? Susan, realizing her sister is

57 - Babette Williams

conspicuously absent, volunteers to take her place. Unfortunately, she's not familiar with how we set up the nametags, so she struggles to find the right tag as people arrive. Sue tries valiantly to make sense of what has become a jumble of overturned nametags. We should have remembered that Ellen is rarely on time.

Meanwhile, the party is swinging. Pirate's Punch has a tendency to sneak up on a person. Even grumps start to feel wonderful. The dance floor is packed. No doubt about it, there's a high ole time going on at the Palace.

At 4 p.m. Aubrey and I walk up to the stage. Aubrey takes the microphone, asks the band to stop playing, and waits until everyone is quiet. With his arm around my waist, he smiles at the crowd and makes an announcement.

"Folks, everyone's been asking us when we were married. The truth is, we haven't had time." Aubrey pauses for an instant to let that message sink in, and continues. "So, we hope you won't mind interrupting this party for a few minutes while we get married."

There are a few moments of confusion. Aubrey adds, "There's one more thing. Please keep drinking and dancing—don't mind us—we'll be married soon."

Then Debbie comes forward, Hugh hands his Dad the ring, Ellen thrusts a bouquet in my hands, and we stand in front of Debbie with our children grouped around us. Debbie handles the ceremony masterfully, although her voice quakes a few times. Aubrey and I keep smiling at each other.

The ceremony is short, and when Debbie pronounces us husband and wife, friends cheer and clap as the groom kisses his bride. The band starts to play, we take to the dance floor, and the festivities continue on a very high note.

At nine o'clock the party winds down, at least at the Palace. About 50 people come back to our house, and we continue drinking and dancing until three in the morning. At that point I ask everyone to please go home as the bride and groom are exhausted.

Then Mr. and Mrs. Williams go to bed. It's been the best surprise wedding I've ever attended.

8.
Now I Lay Me Down to Sleep

One of the first things I did when Aubrey and I were in bed together was break his rib.

We each have our own interpretation of the incident, but we agree that it happened in bed. The "how" is the problem. Aubrey says I have sharp, pointy elbows. I think he is very delicate (especially for a man of his size). In any event, I must have jabbed him? Leaned on him? Poked him?

After the "jab-poke-or-whatever," he became silent. No movement.

Then in a subdued voice, "Babette, I think you broke my rib."

Now I become quiet too. "What do you mean, I broke your rib?"

"Exactly what I said."

"That's impossible. How could I have done that?"

"With your pointy elbow," he answers.

We're silent. It's hard to know exactly what to say when you're in bed with someone and allegedly break his rib. Finally, in my meekest tone, "How do you know it's broken?"

"Because it hurts when I breathe."

There's not much you can do for a cracked rib. Ultimately it heals, but for four to six weeks it hurts to cough or laugh. Aubrey never really complains. Only when he coughs or laughs.

We get past that little mishap and are better at arranging ourselves in bed.

❧❧❧

The honeymoon was interesting. Aubrey said we were going by boat and we'd be on an island. True to his word, we did go by boat. Only thing, it was the *ferry boat* across the St. John's River from A1A to Mayport! The entire trip lasted six minutes. At least I had no time to get seasick.

And now we're home. It's difficult for two older people to adjust but we're trying.

We are both in agreement that breakfast is a time to sip coffee and read the newspaper—unless, of course, we accidentally get into a discussion. Three weeks after our honeymoon, we're talking about eating healthful, nutritious foods, and I comment, "Too bad you don't like spinach salad."

61 - Babette Williams

"Whatever gave you that idea? I do, too, like spinach salad."

"No, you don't," I state. "You told me yourself just the other day you don't like spinach salad."

"When did I say that? I definitely eat spinach salad. I said I like romaine lettuce *better* than spinach. I didn't say I wouldn't eat spinach."

"Aubrey," I reply, "if you prefer romaine lettuce, and you always eat romaine lettuce, then you obviously don't care for spinach salad."

"You don't know what I like. Only I know what I like."

"Yes, I do know what you like. I watch you eat three meals a day, and I have never seen you order a spinach salad."

"That doesn't mean I don't like it. It just means I don't want it right at that moment."

I am beginning to feel testy. I still haven't had my coffee, and we're arguing about spinach salad.

"Aubrey, this is a ridiculous discussion. Who cares if you like or don't like spinach? I don't care if you ever eat a spinach salad."

"Babette, who gives a damn about whether I like spinach salad or not? What is important is that *I* know how *I* feel about spinach, not you."

I turn to him, put my hands on my hips, and announce, "Aubrey, you are the most stubborn, obstinate, hard-headed old man I ever met in my life."

Aubrey looks down at me from his superior height.

Chuckling, he says, "Babette, *I think you need to look in the mirror.*"

He watches as I scowl at the implication, and this heightens his amusement. I draw myself up to my full 5'2."

"What do you mean?" I demand.

"Exactly what I implied. Just call any one of your three daughters and see if they don't think you're stubborn, obstinate, and hard-headed."

I can't believe he said that! I am adjustable, willing to listen, and love change. How dare he!

I pick up the phone to call Ellen, my eldest daughter. The call goes right through and Ellen is delighted to hear from me. I repeat Aubrey's comments, and before I finish my explanation Ellen begins to laugh hysterically.

"Ellen, Ellen, are you there?" I question anxiously. Apparently something has happened in her house or else she didn't hear me very well.

Finally she pulls herself together and says, "Mother, you are funny! Yes, you are adjustable and willing to listen. But you

63 - Babette Williams

are, without a doubt, a very stubborn, obstinate and hard-headed lady."

Aubrey is watching intently. "What did she say?"

I am in no position to answer this question, so I busy myself dialing Susan and pretend I can't hear him.

When she picks up the phone I ask the question again. After a long pause my youngest daughter replies, "Mother, I think there's a germ of truth in Aubrey's statement. You do tend to be positive, and while this is a good trait, it can be interpreted as possibly being stubborn. Also you can be quite adamant."

I can't believe my baby agrees with Aubrey. I pretend Susan is still talking, because I'm not sure what to do next.

"Mother, Mother, are you there? I can't hear you," Sue says.

"I think I'll just call Carol," I murmur.

The connection to Israel isn't very clear. At least I assume that's the reason there is a dead silence after I pose my question the third time. Finally Carol, my middle girl—always measured in her responses and careful with her choice of words—sees fit to reply: "Mom, you had better not look in the mirror."

I hang up the receiver, gather all my courage, and look up at Aubrey. His eyes are warm. He smiles, opens his arms wide and gathers me up.

We laugh.

9.
Fifty of One—Half Dozen of Another

While we're not big talkers at breakfast time, we seem to communicate the best in the morning.

Today Aubrey made a comment. "You know," he said, "I always know what you're thinking even when I don't understand what you're saying."

Now, that's when you're in tune with your mate. I was impressed. We must have a solid marriage—not bad for two stubborn old people. But then I began to digest what he had said. It didn't quite jibe with some happenings in our so-far-short-but-exciting life together.

Last week, as we slipped into our car seats, Aubrey glanced back towards the doorway of the house. He nodded his head,

Dancing in High Cotton - 66

and said, "They definitely would look better if we lowered them."

I see that he's looking at our entrance and reply, "Yes, I totally agree. They shorten the appearance of the house."

Aubrey nods again. "Of course, we could just turn them 180 degrees."

I think about this before responding, "How can you do that?"

He looks at me with a bewildered expression. "It's real easy. I don't want to make any more holes in the brick—just turn them upside down."

"Holes in the brick. Turn them upside down. What on earth are you talking about?"

"The light fixtures on each side of our doorway, of course."

"Oh, the *light* fixtures. I thought you were talking about the *bushes* on each side of our entrance. I couldn't imagine how you would turn them upside down."

"Why would you think I was talking about the bushes when just ten minutes ago, before we came outside, we were discussing whether to lower the sconces on each side of the mirror in the foyer."

"But that was ten minutes ago, and now we're *outside*. What has that to do with sconces?"

"Babette," Aubrey's tone is very patient, "if I had been talking about the *bushes*, I

67 - Babette Williams

would have said *trim* the bushes. You *lower* a light fixture. You *trim* a bush."

Having put an end to what he obviously considers a foolish discussion, Aubrey drives away from the house, satisfied the subject is closed. I mull over our conversation. I should be used to this by now. Aubrey speaks very precisely: he means every single word exactly as he says it.

In direct contrast, I am cavalier, often downright casual, in my choice of words. Aubrey says I'm not accurate—actually very inexact. It's sort of the way we go about hanging pictures. Left to my own devices, I grab a nail, tap it into the wall, and hang the picture. If it isn't right, I do it again. Either way, I'm done in five minutes.

Okay, so he's precise, and I'm a bit more nonchalant. But that doesn't explain why we invariably fail to connect when we make an appointment to meet each other at some place in town. The first time it happened, we thought it was pretty funny. After all, just because I waited at Shoney's for 45 minutes, and he was standing in front of Sonny's Barbecue looking for me . . . These things happen.

The second time left us bewildered. Was the problem that we didn't listen to each other? No, that couldn't be. Both of us are courteous and pay attention. Perhaps we only thought we listened? This is a possibility.

Aubrey, adamant in his belief that he has been precise and accurate, is convinced that I get the gist of his message, and run with it without bothering to hear the details. In my heart I know that he has not been clear in his description.

The latest incident started out simply enough: Aubrey needed to leave his car to have the tires changed, so he asked me to take my car and meet him. I said okay, no problem. We pulled out of our driveway, one behind the other, and I followed him down Fourteenth Street, over the Shave Bridge to George Thrift's Auto. Aubrey went down Fourteenth Street, and turned in at Steve Johnson's Tire Company. I didn't see him pull in, and he didn't see me zoom past.

After waiting 15 minutes in George's parking lot, wondering how Aubrey got lost again, I go into the office. George lets me use his phone to call home, but of course no one answers. Where could he be?

Another 15 minutes pass. No Aubrey. This is so irritating. I go back to the car, shaking my head in exasperation. My husband is always lost. Then I see George Thrift stick his head out, motioning to me to come back. I get out of the car and learn I have a phone call.

69 - Babette Williams

It's Aubrey. "Where are you?" he says. There is a slight edge to his usually pleasant voice.

"I'm at George Thrift's, waiting for you." How could he not know where I am? He just called me.

"But I'm at Steve Johnson's. I *told* you I was getting my tires changed. Where else would I be?"

"I'll be right there, dear," I reply meekly.

Yesterday we did it for the third time. It started the minute we both woke up. After a night's sleep, my body is stiff and achy so that it takes all my willpower to throw off the sheet and blanket, sit up, and actually get going.

"How are you doing?" yells Aubrey. He's in the bathroom, humming away while he shaves.

"I don't think I'll bother to shower today. I just don't feel like it." I'm ashamed to admit the bathroom seems to be seven million miles away.

"Oh, okay," he says, singing away in the shower. Sometimes he's so pleasant and cheerful I find it exhausting.

I hobble to the bathroom. Aubrey is delighted to see me, and says, "I thought you were going to skip your shower."

"I have to take one to loosen up," I mumble. "So far, the only thing working is my mouth."

We move along, enjoy our breakfast, and I get dressed to play golf. "Don't forget we have an appointment in Jacksonville today with the accountant," Aubrey reminds me.

I nod, and ask, "Where should we meet? It's silly for me to come all the way home after golf. I'll change clothes at the club, we can park our cars somewhere in town, and we can go together from there."

"That's a good idea," agrees Aubrey. "Let's meet at the Loop parking lot at 2:15." At least, that's what I thought he said.

Golf was fun, and I finished a bit early, showered, and got to the Loop 15 minutes ahead of time. The lot was fairly empty. I parked and got out of the car so I'd be able to spot Aubrey the minute he pulled in. At 2:15, the time we had agreed to meet, I began to get this sinking feeling. We are both prompt: If we say meet at 2:15, we will each be there at 2:15. I called our house, but there was no answer. Obviously, he was on his way. Relieved, I relaxed against the car, sure he'd be pulling into the lot any second.

Ten more minutes passed—now I *am* concerned. We have an appointment in Jacksonville, which is more than 40 minutes away, at 3:30. Where could he be?

I call the house again. This time Thelma, our housekeeper, picks up the

71 - Babette Williams

phone. She informs me Mr. Williams left before 2 p.m. Where is he?

At 2:45 I am completely frazzled. I call his son, Hugh. Puzzled, Hugh informs me he hasn't spoken to his Dad all day. I decide to tour the entire parking area— maybe he's over by Blockbuster or the Fitness Center, even though we agreed to meet in front of the Loop. Driving slowly, I scan the horizon—there's a car way down at the other end that looks like a large white Chrysler. I see the car begin to back out, heading slowly my way. It's Aubrey.

"You said meet me in the Loop parking lot," I say.

Aubrey looks at me. "Babette, I did not say meet me in the Loop parking lot. What I said was meet me in the Loop parking lot where we always meet people when we go to the football games."

We drive towards Jacksonville, both of us lost in thought. Our first stop is the electronics store. Now Aubrey has a cell phone, and so do I.

10.
Don't Throw Out the Dirty Dishwater Until You Have a New Baby

We've been married for three years and I'm still trying to get our home in order. It's more than a full-time job when you consider men are sloppy and thrive on clutter (well, Aubrey is and does). Although he's immaculate about himself, his belongings are a different story.

For example, the chair outside his bathroom might hold, at any given time, underwear (fresh and used), socks (fresh and used), books (three to six), belts (two to three), and a newspaper article or two from months past. Aubrey is the consummate saver. He doesn't trash anything that might conceivably be of use within the next 30 years.

Dancing in High Cotton - 74

Aubrey tells anyone willing to listen that I spent the past three years working my way through the house, methodically attacking one room at a time. According to my husband, I have totally redecorated, given away, hidden, put in the attic, and thrown out, everything of his that I decided was old and useless.

"Little by little Babette is getting rid of all my old junk," he pronounces. "I am positive that when she gets to the garage and cleans it out, nothing will be left that's old except me. Then I'll be gone, too."

The truth is that my husband doesn't completely trust me. He says I promise over and over again not to throw things out without checking with him, but somehow small items disappear, never to be seen again. I suppose I should be insulted by his mistrust, but deep down I know he's got a tiny little reason to feel the way he does. I cannot forget the Metamucil incident.

But that was three years ago. I guess he's worried because I'm ready to clean out the garage *tomorrow*. You see, everything I took out of the house is now in the attic or the garage. Except for the few times I was lucky and managed to throw stuff away. It's reached the point where we can't get a bicycle in the garage, let alone a car. I have been threatening to do something about it, and Aubrey always agrees that yes, it needs

75 - Babette Williams

to be done, but nothing happens. Aubrey is the world's biggest procrastinator. He says that little trivial details keep getting in the way of important things. I don't see what that has to do with cleaning out the garage, but that's what he says.

So now we're in our grungies, and Aubrey is about to tackle a 30-year accumulation of stuff. The two men I hired to help us were on time, but it only takes half an hour to realize we have a major problem. Aubrey is painstakingly checking each carton, examining every plug, each nail, all the wires, the ropes, every broken tile, before he makes a decision.

We are getting nowhere. Not one shelf has been emptied or straightened. Instead there are piles of debris scattered on the floor. Proceeding in this fashion will result in several months of tedium. Also, I doubt that Aubrey will cheerfully repeat this day.

"Aubrey," I suggest in my kindest voice, "how about our setting up a chair for you outside the garage in the shade. The boys will bring you all the boxes. You can sort through them, and we'll put away what you decide should be saved."

I think Aubrey is relieved. Now all he has to do is say "yes" or "no" in a timely fashion. I stand there watching him toss things into the trash pile. Five hours later we are done. We can actually put our cars in the garage.

My next door neighbor, Sutsy, dropped in on Sunday. She wondered if we were all right, as our cars weren't parked in the driveway. When I told her they were in the garage, she was astounded.

"In all the years we've lived next door, that's the first time the cars were ever put away."

I smiled, quietly acknowledging the brilliance of my performance.

In my heart I know that slowly, no matter how hard I try, the garage will ultimately fill up once more. I figure that with any luck it will take at least ten years—but at that point our children can worry about it.

II.

Woman is a Dog's Best Friend

Some people never learn. I'm one of those people.

I'm at my desk at the Oyster Bay Sales Office when the phone rings. It's George, the young man who installed the Har-Tru tennis courts at our development. He wants to know if Aubrey and I would adopt an eleven-month old male German Shepherd. Emphatically, I tell him NO.

We have Tawny, Tomoka and Dolly. Three dogs are more than enough for any sensible family. (The word "sensible" possibly eliminates the Williams' household.) But George is persistent, pleading with me to take this dog. I tell him NO. The young man doesn't hear clearly—ignoring my NO, he says he's on Barnwell Road, the dog is with him and he'll be right over. Won't I please take a look?

George hangs up the phone before I can say "NO" more decisively. Within one minute the guard gate opens, and sure enough there's George, accompanied by a thin, super-active dog that resembles a German Shepherd, but is unlike any I've ever seen. His legs are longer, his frame is thinner, and his hair feels silky to the touch. He's attractive, but obviously not a pure Shepherd.

George tells me he found the dog running loose near his home three weeks ago. He's run ads in the paper; the dog must've gotten lost but he's well-trained to commands as long as they're spoken in German. But as much as George would like to, he can't continue caring for him. (My German is limited to *geh schlafen*, which my uncle used to say to me when I was a child and he wanted me to go to sleep.) George turns his baby-blue eyes on me and continues: He says he doesn't know where to turn. If he takes the pup to the Humane Society, chances are he'll be put to sleep.

George knows me very well. That's all I have to hear. I don't even want to think about a lovely dog like this being put to sleep. I excuse myself and go into my office to call Aubrey.

"Aubrey, you remember George who built the tennis courts?" Without waiting for a response, I continue, "Well, he's here

79 - Babette Williams

right now with a dog he *says* is a Shepherd, but it doesn't look anything like Tawny or Tomoka. I don't think it's a purebred. Anyway, he wants us to take him."

Aubrey is quiet a moment, then replies, "Well, Tawny is getting frail. We could use another big dog."

I'm silent, thinking about what he said, and then I tell him, "Aubrey, we *really* don't need another dog."

"No, Babette, we don't. *But the dog needs us.*"

Now we're both silent.

"I guess I'll bring him home then."

Of course I'm pleased as can be with Aubrey's answer, which is exactly the response I expect from my husband. I'm positive he'll love our new Shepherd—or whatever the dog is. I know that Aubrey's used to this: Pat was the same way about strays. Aubrey chalks it up to predictable behavior on the part of his mate.

This entire "Save a Dog Saga" began a few months earlier. We were headed home—Aubrey was driving—on Barnwell Road when I spied a gorgeous, perfectly-marked Boston Terrier. Oblivious to the traffic, he was racing towards each passing car and was in danger of being run over. Aubrey jammed on the brakes and brought the car to a screeching halt.

"What're you doing?" I asked.

"Saving gas," he replied.

"What do you mean?"

"You know perfectly well I'd get one mile down this road and you'd make me turn around and go back for the dog. We might just as well pick him up now."

Smiling, because we knew neither of us would ever pass a dog abandoned on the road, we picked up the Boston. Then we began a door-to-door search through each neighboring subdivision in an effort to locate his owners. Meanwhile our new charge covered us with wet kisses, wiggled his body with appreciation, and was totally at ease in his new surroundings.

As we entered the third subdivision more than three hours later, we bumped into a lady who told us, "Oh, that's Bingo. He lives on Marsh Hen Lane, fourth house on the left." Sure enough, two worried adults and one teary child thanked us profusely for rescuing Bingo. We drove home, tired, hungry, and dirty but very happy that Bingo was back with his folks.

Nevertheless, I hated to say good-bye to him. During my lifetime, I've had eight Boston Terriers and am hung up on the breed. Aubrey told me Pat had Boston Terriers, too. This is another in a line of coincidences shared by Pat and me, strengthening my belief that in a previous

81 - Babette Williams

life, somehow Pat and I were linked together.

After Bingo it happened again. I secretly believe that Barnwell Road is now a Mecca for abandoned or lost pets. The word is out that the Good Fairy, alias Babette Williams, will surely rescue the animal.

I spotted a small white dog lying quietly on the side of the road. He didn't even have the energy to look up when I came close.

"Come here, boy," I said softly, holding out my hand, palm up, towards the dog. The lost little guy was an emaciated poodle with button eyes clouded with uncertainty. He wasn't wearing a collar, but I noticed that his nails were clipped, so he'd been well cared for until he got lost. The poor thing had probably been on his own for two or three weeks, judging from his weakened condition.

Tentatively, the poodle got to his feet, slowly coming close enough for me to pet. I waited a few moments for him to gain confidence before I reached out, stopping when my hand was a few inches from his face. He decided I wasn't going to harm him, and his frail little body wiggled with hope. *Was* it hope? I thought so.

I opened my car door and invited him in. He hesitated for the briefest moment, and then tried to hop into the front seat. I gave him a small boost under the rump and

Dancing in High Cotton - 82

he was aboard. Now there were two of us riding down Barnwell Road. The dog seemed happy. I was happy, too. I picked up my car phone to tell Aubrey I had done it again.

No one in Dr. Jim's office was surprised to see me walk in with a new dog. I should stop driving on Barnwell Road—I could avoid all these lost dogs—but Oyster Bay is a peninsula and Barnwell is the only approach to our development.

I left the little poodle, which I named Lucky, and went home. Dr. Jim called the next day to inform us our new addition had heartworm. This is not good—we told Jim to keep him and treat the heartworm, we'd stand the expense. At home Aubrey and I got out another dog dish, brought out two extra dog beds (one for the bedroom, one for the den), and placed ads in the papers, and with the Humane Society, and then we waited.

Ten days later the owner claimed his dog. This time we were out $500 in vet fees, but that was okay. No one ever offered to repay us. But that was okay, too, since we saved Lucky.

And now, here I am again, at Dr. Jim's with Number Three. Jim takes one look at my new charge and exclaims, "Oh, this is an absolutely gorgeous Belgian Malinois. Where on earth did you find him?"

83 - Babette Williams

I look at Jim blankly, and he explains that the Belgian Malinois is a breed similar to the German Shepherd. They are well-balanced, square dogs, elegant in appearance, with short hair and an exceedingly proud carriage. Lighter in build than their German cousins, they are friendly, intelligent, possessing boundless energy and a keen sense of smell. Relatively new to this country, they are becoming popular, particularly as superb narcotics detection and search-and-rescue dogs.

What an interesting turn of events. As Jim talks, I'm examining our new dog, trying to visualize the proud, elegant Belgian Malinois. What I see is an unformed teenager, awkward, giddy and anxious to please. We shall see.

When I get home and tell Aubrey all about it, he immediately goes to the computer and digs up information on the breed. Sure enough, our dog looks exactly like the photos.

Impulsively I suggest, "Let's call him Champ—maybe he'll grow into it." Ha! Was I ever optimistic!

We go through our steps to welcome Champ. Aubrey gets out the extra dog dish, I find two big dog beds, and we struggle to get all four dogs comfortable with each other. Tawny asserts her position—no problem. Tomoka bests the younger dog in a mock fight—no problem. Dolly is again a #%$# pain in the neck.

That little dog just doesn't learn. She is lying on our bed, cuddled up next to me, when Champ sticks his head over the side to ask me for a small affectionate pat. Dolly, annoyed with his intrusion, bares her teeth and goes for Champ—*she'll* show him. All she gets for her trouble is a mouthful of his hair. Champ reacts instinctively to her attack, baring *his* teeth. Unfortunately, he accidentally sinks a canine tooth into the top of Dolly's skull.

It's hard to tell who's more upset. Dolly sits still, stunned, and assumes her most pathetic expression. She is clearly asking, "How could that big brute do this to me?" Champ is abashed. Aw shucks, Mom, I didn't mean to actually *bite* the little critter. Her head just got in the way of my teeth.

And now its six months later, and Champ still has a long way to go before he lives up to his name. On the positive side, he's house-trained, quiet, well behaved, and anxious to please. However, Champ has two annoying traits: He barks incessantly, which we are slowly curing, but worse than that, when we open the front door he dashes through the opening and is *gone*, racing down the street as though he's a Greyhound.

85 - Babette Williams

We understand he isn't running away, he's just *running*. One of us hops in the car and starts looking for him, screaming, "Champ! Champ!" every few minutes.

By the time we give up and come home, Champ is sitting on our doorstep, tail wagging, tongue lolling out the side of his mouth, happy to see us. We cling to the fact that his behavior is improving. Who knows, another year or two, and this shall pass.

Today Walt and Debbie are here from Tallahassee to visit and we proudly show off our new Belgian Malinois. Walt takes one look at Champ and snorts, "A Belgian Malinois! Ha! Why, he looks just like a mutt to me."

I glance at Walt to see if he's kidding, but he isn't. Now I don't care if this dog is a mutt or a champion purebred, I love him, and my feelings are hurt. But I decide not to say anything.

The kids leave, and the next morning Aubrey and I are standing next to each other in front of our bathroom sinks, self-absorbed, brushing and flossing teeth, taking pills, shaving (him), putting on make-up (me). We are having an idle conversation about Champ.

Doing anything first thing in the morning is difficult. All the dogs let us know their needs must be met immediately. Champ has to be petted for at least five minutes; Tomoka starts her guttural half-bark, half-whine meaning, "Let's get the paper NOW"; and Dolly needs her stomach scratched and the door opened so she can saunter into the yard to relieve herself. Only Tawny, the old lady, is secure enough to wait for attention.

"Champ's such a good dog," says Aubrey. "He pushes his way into the bathroom when I'm on the throne just to be petted for a few minutes. Then after I pet him a while, he's satisfied and marches back out. He just wants to know he can come in if he wants to."

I digest this piece of trivia and reply, "I feel bad about Champ. He'd make a great guide dog for the blind, or a drug-detecting police dog. He's sort of wasted living with us. You know, he's not living up to his full potential."

We try to ignore their noise and continue our conversation. Aubrey grins and turns to me, "God forbid the poor dog just relaxes and enjoys his good life!"

Aubrey's comment makes me smile, and I think for the thousandth time how he always puts his finger on what's important. Carefully I climb over and between the four dog beds scattered about our bedroom and head down the hall to the kitchen. I'm going to have a cup of coffee, relax, and enjoy our good life.

12.
Stop the Music–I Want to Get Off

Not all of our days are spent "dancing in high cotton"—Aubrey once explained to me that "dancing in high cotton" is a Southern expression for living high off the hog, and everything is peachy, creamy.

Like any other couple, we have our share of woes, large and small. But the bonus is we have each other.

In November of 1995 I had a mini-stroke and lost the sight in my right eye. After adjusting, the only end result is that I have a hard time reading putts—but then, as the doctor cheerfully pointed out, I always did, so nothing has changed.

The stroke happened a few weeks before we were scheduled to go to Tempe, Arizona, to watch the Gators play in the National Championship. Since we had planned to root for Danny Wuerffel and the entire undefeated team, we decided not to change our plans.

Tempe was fun—that is, until the football game. It was agonizing to watch our Gators get the drubbing of their lives from the much larger and stronger Nebraska Cornhuskers.

The day after the game, 300 sad and sorry Gator fans, including the Williams', leave Tempe for the airport to catch an early afternoon charter flight home. Eight buses filled with orange-clad Gators are confined to the tarmac in a special boarding area to wait for our plane, which is delayed. We wait. And wait. And wait some more.

Six hours later a truck comes by with soft drinks and beer for the marooned travelers. Aubrey takes a few sodas, but I don't feel thirsty, so I refuse a drink. We start boarding the flight after another two-hour wait and take off for home. An hour out of Jacksonville, I begin to feel extremely uncomfortable.

"Aubrey, I don't feel so hot," I say weakly. And then I crumple and faint. My hubby rings for the stewardess, who stretches my limp body out in the aisle. Within seconds there are three doctors hovering over me. I am barely aware that they are checking my pulse, which is sky-high, and giving me water.

89 - Babette Williams

When we land in Jacksonville 40 minutes later, the passengers are told to remain seated until the rescue squad takes me out. Two burly attendants bring in a special little rolling seat that fits between the aisles, and the next thing I know I'm on the gurney being wheeled off the plane and headed for the ambulance. Aubrey gets our car and meets me in the Emergency Room. I'm getting an IV and beginning to feel better. Apparently all that's wrong is that I've dehydrated, which is not uncommon in the desert air, especially if one is an idiot and doesn't drink any water. We get home at 3 in the morning.

"Aubrey," I say as he helps me into bed, "you're right. It's not always easy being a good Gator. But I've been thinking about it, and I don't want you to worry. We'll win the National Championship next year."

He looks at me with love, and yes, admiration. Then he gives me a kiss and a wonderful Aubrey hug.

✂✂✂

One spring morning old Tawny, who has been failing, lay quietly on the floor. She didn't seem able to get up. Dr. Jim came over and while we held her in our arms, he gave her an injection and she left this world. Then our other dogs did a strange thing. When Tawny died, they turned away from her body and left the room. Then, one by one—Tomoka, then Champ, and last, little Dolly—came back, circled around Tawny, sniffed her, and walked away. We knew they were saying good-bye.

But good things were happening for our family, too. Over the next few years we were blessed with more grandchildren. Ellen's two little girls were growing up close by, and Susan had a toddler named Zach in New Jersey. Then along came Sam, born to Carol and Brian.

And in 1998 the Williams' half of our family contributed mightily. Debbie and Walt had Amelia, and three weeks later Anne and Hugh delivered Landyn. We now had *six* grandchildren.

That same year Aubrey was diagnosed with congestive heart failure. True, he had been losing his pep, but we attributed it to "growing old," whatever that means. Now we began to look at health resources on Amelia Island. It didn't take long to realize that if one of us had serious problems, we would have to go to Jacksonville, an hour away.

As luck would have it, about that time the University of Florida sent a flyer describing the CCRC facility to be built near the campus. CCRC? What's that? Continuing Care Retirement Community.

91 - Babette Williams

What's that? Curious, eager to explore a viable solution to comfortable aging without putting a burden on our children, we journey to Gainesville.

We spend several hours with Star, the Sales Representative, and discover Oak Hammock will offer everything we think is important.

First, Shands Hospital is less than ten minutes from the proposed facility, which beats one hour to Jacksonville. If one of us becomes ill, but does not require hospitalization, we would move to either the Assisted Living or Skilled Nursing wing until we recover. A Dementia Wing is in the plans, but I silently decide I don't want to go there.

Now, presuming we're healthy, we'll be able to choose either the formal or casual dining room, depending on our mood. If that doesn't suit us, we can saunter to the Snack Bar, the Ice Cream Shoppe, or better still, the Oak Bar. Star tells us there will be two large indoor pools, a work-out area, a billiards room, and a 250-seat theater. With the exception of the theater, those items don't turn me on. Besides, my head is reeling—so much to think about.

Ground won't be broken for the 138-acre community for several years, so the timing suits our needs perfectly. The clincher is that they allow dogs—we are told we can have a single-family home for our family—ABC and D. (Aubrey, Babette, Champ, and Dolly.)

We are impressed—so impressed that Aubrey and I decide to become Founding Members at Oak Hammock.

13.
Never Judge a Rock Star by His Cover

The insistent barking of our dogs shatters the peace of a Sunday afternoon. Grumbling under my breath, I leave the big rocker on our back porch to investigate. Our home is sheltered by towering live oak trees and is situated far back from the road on a quiet street. It's rare to have an unannounced visitor, especially on Sunday.

The man at our front door startles me. We eyeball each other, which is easy as we're both the same petite size. He's decked out in worn blue jeans, sneakers, and a cut-off tee shirt that exposes several gory tattoos. That's not so bad, but I have trouble accepting the greasy, shoulder-length hair, unshaven face, and squinty eyes partially hidden by granny glasses. Even that might be forgivable. It's his

Dancing in High Cotton - 94

strong beer breath that's proving to be a major distraction.

"Howdy, Ma'am," he says. "I'd like to buy this house."

It takes me a second, but then I remember that yesterday Hugh, our son as well as our realtor, put a *For Sale* sign in our yard.

"Just one minute, please. I'll get my husband," I say firmly, closing the door in his face.

"Aubrey, come quick," I holler. "There's an idiot at the door claiming he wants to buy the house. His breath reeks of alcohol. Get rid of him *right away*." I realize this is strange advice when you consider that I am a former realtor who always preached, "You can't tell a book by its cover."

But it's perfectly clear to me that this *person* could not afford a chicken coop, let alone a substantial house in a family-oriented neighborhood. Aubrey, always obliging, heads for the door.

Five minutes pass, then ten minutes. By the end of 15 minutes, I'm unable to stand the suspense. I peer through the glass panel of the front door and see my husband with his arm around the pipsqueak's neck and they're laughing and talking like old friends. Not only that, they're walking towards the *house.*

95 - Babette Williams

"Babette, I've agreed to show Billy Jones our house, if you don't mind." Aubrey looks at me with a peculiar expression that I translate as, "This is okay. Trust me." I paste a smile on my face.

"Fine," I reply through clenched teeth. "Do come in."

"Babette, Billy was part of The Leonard Skinner Band." *Aubrey acts as if this should explain everything. I suppose it would, if I only knew who Leonard Skinner was.*

"Oh." I smile blankly.

"Ma'am, do you mind if I bring my woman in?" Billy asks.

"Of course not." After all, what can I say when Aubrey obviously knows something significant about Billy Bob (my nickname for him) that I don't. Billy goes out to the car, a dirty, tired-looking sedan, and returns with his woman in tow.

"This is Maxine. We're fixin' to be married."

She's a large woman, larger than Aubrey who weighs close to 250 pounds, and very tall. However, she's well groomed and attractively dressed. The contrast between Billy Bob and Maxine is awesome.

Everybody smiles and Maxine makes a startling disclosure.

"I know you, Aubrey. I went to school a few years behind your son, Hugh. My name was Maxine Richards, Sherman Richards' daughter."

The plot is thickening. Maybe this Billy person is who he says he is. And maybe they are looking for a house if in fact he's "fixin'" to marry a local. Feeling bewildered, I take Aubrey aside.

"Who is Leonard Skinner?" I hiss.

"Babette, I can't believe you never heard of Lynyrd Skynyrd. It's not a *he*; it was a famous rock band, spelled L-Y-N-Y-R-D S-K-Y-N-Y-R-D." (Aubrey's expression is incredulous as he patiently spells out the letters for his poorly educated wife.) "Most of the members were killed in a plane crash some years ago. Billy says he didn't make the flight."

The atmosphere warms up. Aubrey gives Billy Bob several shots of bourbon. They choose some rock music from Aubrey's extensive collection. Billy Bob picks up Dolly, our tiny Mini-Dachshund, and dances around the living room with her. Dolly doesn't seem to mind his bad breath. Maxine starts to dance; I join her. After all, we have to be friendly.

They ask to see the house so I take Maxine, and Aubrey escorts Billy.

"I want the house," says Maxine. "It's going to be my wedding present. Billy is a rock star, and he has 4.8 million in the bank."

I nod but I'm not a believer. She continues. "I'd like all the furnishings, too. They're perfect and that way I won't have to do a thing except move in."

"I guess I could, but I'd have to figure out their worth. Everything in the house has been chosen specifically to fit our rooms."

"We have to get out of our condo by the end of July. Could we be in by August first?"

I gulp. That's barely seven weeks away.

We have a few more drinks, and Billy asks if he can bring in Susie, which turns out to be his guitar. Susie looks old and beat up, too.

The four of us, plus Dolly, sit around the breakfast room table for a brief discussion. We tell them the asking price for the house is $895,000, expecting some bargaining. Billy assures us price is not a problem, and adds that he'll pay cash the next day. We agree not to bother with a deposit—we're only talking about a few hours. With that, the odd duo depart, promising to return in the morning.

As soon as the door closes, we call our son, Hugh. And the shock sets in. Are they for real? Are we in fact about to sell our house just a few days after it's been put on the market? How can we move out so fast?

Dancing in High Cotton - 98

Aubrey and I have dinner and shortly thereafter go to bed. My head is spinning, either from excitement or liquor, not that it matters.

"See, Babette, it's just like you always say. You can't judge people by their clothes. It's so funny that you turned them away."

"Thank heaven you were smarter," I apologize.

The next morning we agree we'll never hear from Billy and Maxine again. It's too good to be true. It was probably a hoax, and we aren't going to think any more about it.

The telephone rings shortly after breakfast. Hugh wants to know if he can bring Maxine and Billy over at 10 to write up a contract. Now we're ecstatic. It *is* true. We are in a total dither.

Promptly at 10 the bell rings. This time I go to the door with a *real smile* on my face. We've sold our house, bing bang boom— just like that.

Billy Jones looks marginally better. Even though he has on the same outfit, he has washed and shaved. His breath smells almost normal, a mixture of peppermint mouthwash tinged with a slight hint of beer. Under the circumstances, this can be overlooked.

Hugh has prepared a contract, but no one has time to address it, least of all Billy. He's having some bourbon and wants to

99 - Babette Williams

dance with Dolly again. Maxine and I quietly go through the house listing the furniture that we'll be keeping so there's no misunderstanding when we write up the details of the contract.

Billy disappears, but returns in a moment with his guitar. "This is a Les Paul guitar," he tells Hugh, pride evident in his voice. Politely, Hugh examines the guitar, and then hands it back to Billy.

"I notice it's not strung," Hugh comments.

"Oh, no, I never keep it strung." Billy shrugs off Hugh's comment and leaves the room again. We hear him in the hall, talking to Thelma. She's been with our family for over fifteen years. The sound of Thelma's giggle is punctuated by several "Yes, Sirs," and Billy and Thelma reappear in the kitchen. Billy has his arm over Thelma's shoulders—she's small, too.

"Thelma's going to work for me," he advises us. Thelma is grinning widely, which tells me one thing: unlike the lady of the house, *she knows* who The Lynyrd Skynyrd Band was.

Finally we sit down at the table. Billy speaks. "The house is $900,000, right?"
I politely correct him: "It's $895,000."

Billy either doesn't hear me, or it doesn't register. "I'll give you a million dollars for the house and all the furniture. Will that do it?"

I smile sweetly. "Why, Billy, that's the exact number we had in mind."

With that we all shake hands, and it's a done deal. Hugh finishes the contract, which all of us sign.

"July 29th is my birthday," Billy tells us.

"Why, that's interesting. Hugh's birthday is August 1st, mine is August 7th, and Aubrey's is August 17th," I contribute.

"We ought to have a party," the future owner of our house declares.

"Okay, let's do it. Let's celebrate our birthdays and we'll give a farewell party for us and a welcome party for you." I'm really agreeable. After all, *tomorrow* this man is going to pay us *one million dollars*.

Billy thinks about the party. Then he leans towards me and confides, "There's only one thing, I have to have my favorite food. It's a tuna fish sandwich and French fries."

"No problem," I reassure him. "A tuna fish sandwich and French fries it is."

"There's one other thing," Billy adds. "I'll bring the band. They might look a little rough."

"No problem," Aubrey chimes in. "We can handle it."

Satisfied on all counts, Maxine and Billy depart.

101 - Babette Williams

We cannot believe the events of the day. How could it be this easy? Later, we sleep like two rocks, or do I mean rock *stars*, confident that tomorrow will see us one million dollars richer.

Even though I hate to cook, the first thing I do on Tuesday morning is prepare a huge tuna salad, and cut up potatoes so that they are ready for the frying pan when our guests arrive.

About ten o'clock we begin to feel anxious. Around ten-thirty Aubrey has an idea. "I think I'll try to contact Billy on his cell phone."

A couple of minutes later, I ask, "What did he say?"

Aubrey sounds glum. "The phone is not receiving calls at the present time."

At eleven, Hugh calls. We tell him about the cell phone. He has no news to report, either. At twelve we are downright concerned. Perhaps Billy had an accident on the way to the bank. God forbid.

By one o'clock we reluctantly decide to have lunch. I refuse to touch Billy's tuna fish. Surely he'll show up. Undoubtedly he had trouble with the bank. Or maybe he's in the hospital. Hopefully it's not fatal.

The afternoon drags on. Hugh calls the condo where Maxine and Billy are staying. No one is registered under that name.

"Dad, you know that guitar that Billy said was a Les Paul?" Hugh asks.

"Yes," Aubrey acknowledges. .

"Well, Dad, that was no more a Les Paul Guitar . . . It was just a cheap replica."

Aubrey is silent. After graduating from college, Hugh spent two years at the Guitar Institute in Hollywood. Then Aubrey says, "The fact he doesn't keep it strung makes me think he can't play."

Meekly I suggest that perhaps it's a hoax. Maybe we should've gotten rid of them on Sunday afternoon. No, we argue with ourselves. How do you account for Maxine? She's definitely real. Hugh confirmed that. Aubrey knew her father. Too bad he's dead or we could've checked with him. Surely we'll hear from them tomorrow.

But we don't, nor the next day, or the day after that.

On Friday I play golf with my friend, Mary, and I relay this strange chain of events. She looks at me with a peculiar expression.

"You know, Babette, that's really funny." Mary is a mortgage broker and knows all the realtors in town. "Yesterday I heard about a couple exactly fitting this description who looked at a very expensive property in Yulee, signed a contract, and never showed up again."

103 - Babette Williams

I promptly hook my drive to the left. The ball soars into the marsh, lost forever.

When I get home, I repeat Mary's comment to Aubrey.

"Well, it sure was fun while it lasted." I manufacture a smile for Aubrey's benefit.

"Ah, Babette, it was just too easy."

I nod at my mate. Unfortunately, it looks as though my instincts about Billy Bob were on the money.

The next morning I throw out the tuna salad.

14.
Snug Harbor

Incredibly, one month after the Billy Bob episode, we have a bona fide excellent contract on our house. Now what? The contract gives us three months to vacate, which seems like a lot until you consider we haven't a clue where to move.

"I hate to give up the water," Aubrey says thoughtfully. "Maybe we can find a small house near Gainesville for the interim time." Oak Hammock, our eventual destination, was still very much in the planning stage.

We agree that what we want is a small waterfront getaway within an hour of what will be our primary home in Gainesville, with no upkeep and plenty of privacy. Once, while Aubrey and I were visiting friends in Crystal River on the west coast of Florida, we became enchanted with the laid-back atmosphere of the small town. The crystal clear, spring-fed waters of Kings Bay, which flowed into the salt water of the Gulf of Mexico, would make boating and fishing accessible to us. We were amazed to find a place reminiscent of life in rural America in the forties.

Now Aubrey and I make a return trip to Crystal River, just to look around. We enjoy a marvelous breakfast at an "old timey" restaurant called the Paradise Diner. We cannot believe that for $2.95 we each have two eggs, bacon or sausage, two hot cakes, grits, biscuits, and all the coffee we can handle.

We leave the diner, and a wild impulse seizes us. We stop at a real estate office where a man on floor duty, occupied in picking his teeth, sizes us up.

"May I help you?" he says half-heartedly, not removing the toothpick.

Since I'm the one with real estate experience, I speak up. "We're looking for a getaway home and have just three prerequisites," I state firmly. "The house must be on water, give us privacy, and have no grass to cut."

The realtor yawns, and finally drawls, "I'm going to turn you over to another agent. He knows all the water property."

Since all the property in Crystal River has a close connection with water, it is apparent he wants to be rid of us. Good. I didn't like him, either.

A second realtor walks towards us. This one is named Steve. We repeat our request. He thinks for a minute and says, "I have exactly one property that meets your needs. Let's go."

In five minutes we've left his office, drive on the main highway for a few miles, and end up in an out-of-the-way corner just a half mile away. Miller Creek Road, a country lane, winds through dense virgin swampland protected by the state of Florida.

Steve stops the car. We glimpse an oddly-shaped dark-brown stilt house among the trees, barely visible from the road.

Gingerly we navigate a rickety walkway through low swampland that spans the 100-feet distance to the house. In places the walk barely clears the swamp. I can't help but wonder if there are alligators, but I put this thought out of my mind. (Sort of.)

We love the unusual twelve-sided shape of the house, the quaint setting, and the huge windows facing the large natural spring that flows into the Gulf of Mexico. In effect, this is the backyard. There's deep water for the boat, a plethora of wildlife: birds, fish, manatees, dolphin, and yes, even alligators. Plus complete solitude, and *no lawn to mow.*

Dancing in High Cotton - 108

We are falling passionately in love with the property. It has taken all of ten minutes.

We write a contract that includes the furniture, with one stipulation: we can legally replace the skinny spiral staircase with an elevator, as neither of us can handle the winding steps.

Two weeks later all approvals are in place and we own the "Swamp House."

We have three months to whip this wonderfully located, but sorely neglected, house into shape. Fortunately we find a contractor able to attack our project with vigor.

As planned, and on time, Aubrey and I strut up a new, completely enclosed substantial boardwalk covered by a metal roof. The walk is enclosed with closely-spaced boards so that Dolly can't fall overboard.

From the porch a new boardwalk leads to the dock, with a ramp to the floating portion. Our pontoon boat sits there ready to carry up to 16 people.

But the piece de resistance: I ask you, how many dogs have their own private "Poop Deck?" Champ and Dolly had nowhere to go to relieve themselves until Aubrey came up with the idea of an enclosed pen extending into the swamp from the boardwalk. By adding dog doors so

109 - Babette Williams

they could come and go at will, and putting tons of sand for a base over the swampy ground, he created an ideal situation. We, or rather they, christened the Poop Pen very promptly. Unfortunately it became my task to clean it out daily.

With that final addition, the Williams' are ecstatic, and two days before closing on the Amelia Island house, we're on our way to our new home in Crystal River.

15.
I've Found My Buttons

When she was exactly two months old we brought her home. She weighed five pounds: a perfect little Boston Terrier puppy. I'd been watching the newspaper for six months, ever since Dolly passed away at 15, until I noticed an ad offering three puppies. Chassahowitzka is a town smaller than Crystal River (if that's possible) and it's only ten minutes away. No wonder it's so small—the name is too hard to spell and impossible to pronounce.

"Aubrey, let's go for a ride," I suggested.

"Okay. Where to?" My mate is always amiable.

"Well, there's a litter of puppies just a few minutes from here."

"Oh."

I wait and then say hesitantly, "Want to?"

In my heart I know Aubrey would like another big dog like Champ, but I miss something to cuddle. Especially since I know I face the loss of my daughter, Carol, in the very near future. I need all the help I can get.

"Sure, honey," he says, lifting himself out of the chair. "Let's go."

"I'm not going to *get* a puppy. I just want to *look* at them," I explain.

"Sure," he replies. "I understand."

⚜⚜⚜

We are escorted into a fenced-in yard to watch the babies play. The mother is friendly and heaves herself up and over to the shade, glad of a chance to rest. The puppies are fat, healthy, and obviously well-cared for.

One puppy catches my attention. It's her expression: she's so interested in everything we do and it seems to me she's trying to figure it out. After a few minutes she trots over to my feet and sits down. I imagine I look huge to her, so I plop down on the grass. She takes my action as an invitation and sidles onto my lap, covering my face with kisses. What a smart dog.

We thank the breeder profusely and depart. True to my promise, we don't take a puppy.

I'm in a dither. I want her. Do I want her? Is she the one? I won't say a word until I've figured it out, I decide. We stop for dinner.

As we relax and enjoy our drinks, my husband speaks. "Let's name her Bitsy."

I'm taken aback, but of course I should've known better.

"What makes you think we're taking the puppy? How can you name her?"

"Oh, I know we're going back for her tomorrow, so she might as well have a name."

The next day Bitsy Buttons rides home in my arms.

cXcXcX

She proves to be everything we want in a puppy, but more so. We expect her to eventually weigh about 13 pounds, maybe 15 at the utmost. As time passes, she grows, and grows, and at six months is still *growing*. She's not fat. It's just that her legs are like stilts and she is one big muscle. I begin to believe she'll be the tallest Boston in the world. Who knows, maybe she'll make The Guinness Book of Records. Worried, I check her papers. Boston Terrier on both sides, no doubt about it.

We drop the Bitsy. It no longer fits.

16.

God Grant Me Courage

My middle daughter, Carol, is being buried in Westchester County, New York, after a courageous two-year battle with cancer. It is unthinkable that Aubrey and I are at the cemetery attending her funeral: how could she have passed away before me?

As the final amen is whispered by our small group of mourners, a gust of wind rustles the leaves on the stately oak tree that shades her gravesite, surprising us on this mild April day. Perhaps it is Carol's way of saying a last goodbye. Quietly we walk back up the gentle slope to the road where the limousines wait, and as we settle down in our seats I unexpectedly recall a dream I had several years ago.

In this dream, I am the one who dies, and my will specifies my body be cremated and the ashes sent in turn to each of my three daughters, Ellen, Susan, and Carol, for a four-month period. Now this in itself is noteworthy, because I have always assumed that following my funeral, I'd be buried in Aubrey's family plot, just one-half mile from our home. When the subject comes up in conversation I seem to avoid the topic by putting it off "for the future."

In my dream, no funeral is held. The ashes are shipped directly after cremation by parcel post from Fernandina Beach to my eldest daughter, Ellen, and her husband, Steve, in Houston. Ellen opens the carton and carefully unpacks the protective heavy brown wrapping paper. I can visualize her shocked expression when she sees the chocolate-colored plastic container the size of a cigar box.

"My goodness," she murmurs, turning the container from side to side, "this urn is disgraceful! My mother had dash and spirit. She can't be in a container as plain and shabbily made as this!"

She heads for La Galleria, Houston's finest shopping district, and dashes into Tiffany's. The manager recognizes Ellen, and when she explains the purpose of her visit, he settles her in a private booth and begins to assemble some possible selections.

Several hours later she decides on a delicate, well-proportioned robin's egg blue

117 - Babette Williams

cloisonné vase. It stands ten inches tall, four inches at the neck, widening to eight inches in the belly and narrowing again at the base. Small Chinese horses in battle armor, and their riders in flowing capes, are outlined in gold filigree. At the store manager's suggestion she adds a carved mahogany pedestal.

"There," she says with satisfaction, "That's more like it! I'll put this on my mantel and I can enjoy thinking about my mother all the time."

At the end of her designated four-month period as caretaker, Ellen hires a professional packer to carefully crate the vase for its journey east to Susan, my youngest daughter, who lives in Upper Montclair, New Jersey, with her husband, Bruce, and son, Zach. Susan is thrilled to have her turn with her mom, and she and Bruce struggle to undo the solid wood container.

"My goodness," Susan murmurs when the urn is revealed, "this is a valuable piece of art. I had no idea." Without a word, they sit down in the living room. Then Susan speaks: "Bruce, we'd better make sure no one takes it or breaks it."

She worries about the vase all evening, and in the middle of the night, picturing the vase sitting exposed on their dining room sideboard, she has the solution.

"I'll store it in a safe hiding place in the basement where no one can find it. My mother would expect me to take good care of such a valuable antique."

She hops out of bed, nudging Bruce to get up and help her. Before he has a chance to waken or get out of bed, she carts the urn off to the basement, wraps it in several burlap bags, and hides it under two old suitcases in a corner.

At the end of her four-month stint, Susan goes down to the basement and is relieved to find the urn resting comfortably where she has hidden it. She lovingly repacks the vase in the tissue paper, brown wrapping paper, and shavings she had saved, places it back in the crate, and sends it overseas to Carol, my middle daughter.

Carol, Brian, and their son, Sam, live in Israel where Brian heads the United Nations Relief Association for the Middle East. Carol was anticipating her turn with her beloved mother's ashes, and when the crate arrives in Herzliya at long last, she unpacks it in a hurry, Sam squatting at her side.

"This is a work of art," Carol muses, studying the intricate design and beauty of the vessel. Holding the vase in two hands, she walks over to her living room bookcase, and places it on the top shelf, safely out of Sam's reach.

Early the next morning Carol sets off by herself, driving her VW station wagon through the coastal tree-lined streets of Herzliya. She has strapped the vase next to her in Sam's baby seat. Her destination is the Judean hills.

Two hours later Carol stops the car at a friend's Arabian horse ranch. She disappears inside the barn, and 20 minutes later is back at the car, leading a chestnut mare by the bridle. She retrieves the vase and fits it inside the saddlebag behind the saddle on the mare's back.

Once mounted, she quickly starts to trot, and then gallop, towards the Judean hills. The chestnut mare is now flying at full speed, tossing sand everywhere. Carol feels the wind in her face and senses the image of her mom riding beside her as they did several years before, racing with abandon, smiling with joy at the utter freedom.

Carol is now at the highest point of land overlooking Jordan and Israel. Sitting absolutely still on the mare, Carol absorbs the brilliant sunshine and sees the vibrant blue sky. My mother loved this, Carol remembers. She dismounts and slowly takes the vase out of the saddlebag. Then, tucking her arm through the reins, she unfastens the wooden stopper.

"My mom would hate being shut in a dark tight spot," Carol says aloud. "She was a free spirit!" Carol releases the remains, weeping and smiling as the breeze scatters the ashes in a thousand directions.

✂✂✂

For me, this has been an unbearably long and difficult two-year period. And now Carol, my special middle daughter, has left this world. I know that we just buried her body in Westchester. But her spirit—that's a different story. No one can take away the memories I cherish of her extraordinary life, or the bonds we shared as mother and daughter. And I think: I brought her into this world and, fittingly, I was there to help her make the transition to the next life.

But perhaps the deepest comfort of all is the certainty in my heart that Carol will be waiting for me when it is my turn to leave this earth, and we will share again that incomparable and glorious sense of riding together into the wind.

17.
Old Folks at Home

A wise friend told me that I'd never get over Carol's death, but that I would, in time, learn to live with the loss. Only a few months have passed and I'm struggling on a daily basis. I see her when I'm driving, when I listen to the radio, walking the dogs: her presence is constant.

Carol died in my arms at 1:30 in the afternoon. That night Brian, Sam, my daughter Ellen, and I went to dinner at Carol's favorite Italian restaurant. We're deep into spaghetti when Ellen says, "I feel as though my sister's right here."

Sam, age eight, looks up from his plate. "I know what you mean, Aunt Ellen," he says. "I feel my mother is here with us, too."

When we get back to their house, Sam points to the sky. "Grandma, do you see that very bright star? The really bright one? That's my mom. I know it is."

It's a comforting thought even now, and I cling to it.

※※※

Our house at Oak Hammock is almost finished and we're scheduled to move in June. I'm grateful for all the planning required—it's keeping me busy.

Today we're going to Gainesville for the Founding Members' Welcome Party at the Commons Building at Oak Hammock. The building reminds me of a five-star hotel in its elegance. A three-piece choral group is playing elevator music. The atmosphere is friendly, and we nod, introduce ourselves to others, sip the wine, and taste the goodies.

"Aubrey, I feel funny. Get me out of here," I whisper.

"What's the matter?" Aubrey is at my side, guiding me to the door.

"I don't know . . . I feel queasy, as though I may faint."

We make it through the front door without a mishap and head for our car. I am fighting a terrible sensation, but can't describe it. I start to tremble.

"I don't like it here. I don't belong here. Everyone's *old*. I'm not ready to be an inmate."

I start to cry. Aubrey is beside himself. But so am I. What on earth is happening to me?

123 - Babette Williams

"Maybe we should stay in Crystal River. I love it there. We're happy. What are we doing here?"

We're in the car, driving around Gainesville, trying to regroup. Suddenly I start to giggle.

"Maybe we can be the trustees, since we're going to live in a house, not an apartment in the Commons. And we can go to the Big House for dinner."

Aubrey is visibly relieved to see me brighten up but feels the temporary breakdown, which is unlike me, deserves discussion.

"Honey, listen. We don't have to move. You know that. But I think you had a reaction to some of the older folks at the gathering. And maybe a feeling of claustrophobia, of being penned in."

"No, I think I realized that this will be our last move. And it frightened me."

Of course I get over my nervous attack, or whatever it is, and plunge into the move to Oak Hammock. Not a moment to soon, as things turn out. Almost immediately Aubrey ends up in the hospital with internal bleeding. It's the start of a year-long battle to stop the bleeding and restore his quality of life.

In October, tired of being called "Lurch," I decide to finally get a long overdue knee replacement. And again Oak Hammock proves to be the right place. One week in the skilled nursing venue, plus daily therapy right here on premises—who can beat that?

I begin to realize that all the residents have to make the same adjustments that we do. We are terrified of giving up our independence, of becoming ill and a burden. But we've moved to Oak Hammock so our children won't have to cope with the problem of aging parents in need of care. Now that we're settled, we discover our horizon is expanded through new friends and the multitude of activities offered at Oak Hammock. We haven't "given up" anything—rather we've gained.

We've been fortunate in forging a strong friendship with the two couples that live nearest to us. Impromptu get-togethers for cocktails, going to the Big House for dinner, all on the spur of the moment. And we are gradually meeting more folks that we enjoy.

Champ and Buttons have adjusted far more readily. Our cul-de-sac is the "in place" to live if you are a dog. All of us have at least one; some residents, like us, have two. Little Buttons, barely one year old, is the youngest kid on the block. Little is probably not the correct description as she now weighs twenty pounds.

She is playful, funny, very loving, and wants only to be with us. When we're home,

125 - Babette Williams

Buttons is angelic. However, when we leave her, even though Champ is home, she gets to work chewing up pillows, shag rugs and furniture. Her latest craze is electronics—she managed to mutilate a cell phone and a garage opener in one sitting. And now we note she has become a gourmet. Her preference is filet of sole (as in shoes).

Champ must cringe watching her demolish forbidden property. Her *largest* coup was an 8 x 10 shag rug: she whittled it down so neatly that it is now 4 x 6. I guess I'll throw it away—the sides are a little uneven.

Buttons knows every security guard at Oak Hammock. She should. At the slightest opportunity she bounds out of the house, madly seeking excitement. We call Security and jump into the car, chasing after our puppy that has suddenly developed the speed of a greyhound.

We needn't have worried. In a few minutes a golf cart heads our way with Buttons sitting regally in the driver's lap. She doesn't even have the grace to look ashamed. Instead she kisses her benefactor in the ear, and returns to the Williams'.

We know her antics will ebb as she becomes older. However, we decide to deal with her "escape artist"-style, and install an electric fence around our yard. Champ catches on immediately and knows that the

Dancing in High Cotton - 126

flags signify danger. Not his little sister. The first time she's out, she bounds through the unseen fence, screams like a banshee and heads down the road. True to form, within a few minutes she arrives home in style, but we can't get her out of the security cart. No way is she going to risk being stung again.

ᚼᚼᚼ

Yesterday Aubrey got a good lesson in "Life Ain't Always Fair." It started several days ago when I was taking Ellen to the local airport, proudly tooling my car like a pro.

"Ellen, did you know that I've never gotten a ticket in my life?" (When will I *ever* learn?)

As I'm making my statement, I turn right onto Airport Road. Without thinking I cross into the middle lane. Unfortunately, I fail to notice that a car coming from the other direction also had the right to turn. I avoid hitting him by swerving back into the proper lane. Then I see flashing yellow lights.

"Looks like someone's going to get a ticket," I smirk to Ellen.

And then I realize he wants *me* to pull over. I do. Ellen slinks lower in her seat and says, "Oh, shit." (Under her breath.)

127 - Babette Williams

I jump out of the car and zip back to see the cop. He's huge, maybe 6'5".

"Officer, I apologize. I was wrong. I was an absolute idiot." I know I'm babbling but can't stop. "I know better than to make a turn and go into the second lane. I'm so glad I didn't hit you. You should give me a ticket. I absolutely deserve one. I'm so embarrassed." I probably would've kept on for an hour, but he finally got a word in.

"You know that was illegal—it was a bad move."

I nod my head.

"Let me see your driver's license." He studies the document. And then the most amazing thing happens! My policeman *laughs*. And then he hugs me.

"I'm not going to give you a ticket, lady," he says, smiling at me. "Please, just don't be careless again." With that, he shakes my hand, and gets back into his car.

Yesterday we were on our way to Jacksonville and the route we follow goes through Waldo, a small town famous as a speed trap. Aubrey is following all the signs warning drivers to slow down. I guess he missed one, though, because a local police car is bearing down on us, flashing yellow lights. Sighing, we pull over.

I whisper to Aubrey, "I can't imagine why he stopped you. You weren't doing anything wrong. I know you slowed down."

Why are all cops so large? This one lumbers up, peers in at Aubrey, and says, "May I see your license and registration, sir?" There is no discussion, no hugging, no smiling. Within seconds he writes a speeding ticket.

"You know you were going way over the limit," he says. I keep quiet, but I'm dying to tell him that my husband was *not* speeding. Instead, I bite my tongue.

This week Aubrey has been on his computer completing the remedial course for speeders. As I say, "Life ain't fair sometimes."

❧❧❧

Someone asked me how I feel about life at Oak Hammock. My answer?

"I love it here. I just don't love that we're here."

I don't know how or when we got "old." I don't feel any different and think maybe "old" is a misnomer. True, we're aging, as is everyone around us. But we totally enjoy life on a daily basis. Besides the new friendships formed in the community, our largest blessing is the warmth and love of our combined family.

And today is a most special day. Brian and Sam will be arriving at any moment. They are going to live in Gainesville, just a

129 - Babette Williams

ten minute drive from Oak Hammock. Brian felt that without Carol, he and Sam would prosper by having the support of family, so he decided to sell their New York State home, and "go south." We cannot believe our good fortune.

From now on, "Poppy" Aubrey and I will accompany Sam to football games, attend soccer games, take him swimming, and relish being part of his life.

We will delight in every single day we have together by laughing, sharing, and above all, loving one another.

LaVergne, TN USA
09 January 2011
211679LV00002B/1/A